entering
the
kingdom

entering the kingdom

a fresh look at conversion

Edited by
MONICA HILL

MARC Europe
British Church Growth Association

British Library Cataloguing in Publication Data

Entering the kingdom.
1. Conversion
I. Hill, Monica
248.2'46   BV4916

ISBN 0–947697–34–9 (MARC Europe)
0–948704–05–5 (BCGA)

MARC Europe is an integral part of World Vision, an international humanitarian organisation. MARC's object is to assist Christian leaders with factual information, surveys, management skills, strategic planning and other tools for evangelism. MARC also publishes and distributes related books on mission, church growth, management, spiritual maturity and other topics.

The British Church Growth Association is a co-ordinating body for those interested in the growth (spiritual, numerical, organic and incarnational) of the British church today. It comprises researchers, teachers, consultants and practitioners who share information, insights, experience, and new thinking through regional and national activities, a regular journal, occasional publications and other resources, seminars and conferences. It is located at 59 Warrington Road, Harrow, Middlesex HA1 1SZ.

table of contents

entering the kingdom

a fresh look at conversion

1
entering the kingdom — then and now

MONICA HILL

Word origins

'Conversion' is often thought of as an old-fashioned term. In fact the opposite is true; in its present understanding, it is an invention of the modern church. The term 'conversion' — although appearing in Hampole's Psalter[1] as long ago as the fourteenth century and despite occasional references in succeeding centuries[2] — only came into regular use during the last century through the American Revival Movement.

The word 'conversion' was, in fact, coined by Jonathan Edwards, the father of modern crusade evangelism, when he used it to refer to decisions for Christ made at revival meetings. The men behind the mass evangelistic meetings in the mid-nineteenth century believed that one could plan and organise revival. Hence even today the term 'revival' is used in different ways in America and Britain. In Britain it generally denotes a fresh movement of the Holy Spirit — an activity of God — whereas many Americans speak of revival in organisational terms — as an activity of man.

If we are to understand the term 'conversion', we need to recognise its contextual roots within the revivalist meetings of nineteenth-century American evangelicalism. But even more essentially we need to examine the biblical concept from which it is derived. The danger with the use of a modern term that does not stem directly out of a biblical concept is that the term may then be used to redefine the biblical concept — rather than the biblical concept being used as the norm for defining the modern term. The biblical concept underlying the term 'conversion', as we shall see, is that of entering the Kingdom.

Biblical conversion

Jesus did not speak of 'conversion'; neither do any of the New Testament writers, although the term 'convert' is used in I Timothy 3:6 in reference to the qualifications for eldership: 'He must not be a recent convert.' As a matter of historical fact, all members of the Early Church were converts as they had belonged to other faiths before receiving Christ. But conversion as we think of it today is not mentioned in the Bible.

Jesus speaks of 'repentance', 'belief', and 'entering the Kingdom'. Both Mark and Matthew record that Jesus began his ministry in Galilee in terms very similar to John the Baptist: 'The time has come. The kingdom of God is near. Repent and believe the good news!' (Mark 1:15). Jesus also taught the necessity for spiritual rebirth. In his reply to Nicodemus he said, 'I tell you the truth, unless a man is born again, he cannot see the kingdom of God' (John 3:3). Thus, in Jesus' teaching, repentance, belief and spiritual rebirth are prerequisites of 'entering the Kingdom'.

Repentance

The term 'repentance' comes from the Greek word *metanoia* (noun) which comes from the verb *metanoieo*, defined as 'to undergo a change in frame of mind and feeling, to repent'.[3] This was basic to the message of the prophets who continually called a rebellious generation back to a commitment to God. They called for a radical change in men's attitudes and actions, for a turning away from oppression, injustice, immorality and idolatry. Thus the teaching of Jesus was both a fulfilment — and a development — of the message of the prophets of ancient Israel. He called men to turn away from the values and lifestyle of the world and towards the values of the Kingdom.

A true view of repentance would mean a total change in lifestyle, values and commitment. Commitment to God overrides all other commitments and loyalties. We make a U-turn — turn our back on the world and our face towards God.

John's message of repentance, when accepted by the people, led immediately to baptism in water. 'Repent and be baptised.' The tears of repentance were necessary before baptism. Repentance meant turning away from the past and making a new beginning, seeing the whole of life from a new perspective — God's perspective. 'The past, however apparently blameless before, begins to be revalued, even rewritten. The convert will see his newly-found identity and response to Christ as real; all that previously kept him from it as shadowy, false and empty.'[4]

Belief

Jesus speaks about believing the good news. In this sense belief means acceptance of the message that he proclaimed. That message not only proclaimed the call to repentance but also the good news of the forgiveness of sins. 'Friend, your sins are forgiven' was the simple message that Jesus conveyed to the paralytic brought to him for healing (Luke 5:20). Jesus used this incident to teach 'that the Son of Man has authority on earth to forgive sins' (Luke 5:24).

Belief meant also believing the good news that Jesus was the Son of God, the Messiah, the Saviour, the Teacher, the Way to holiness and eternal life. It was the good news of the Kingdom which God was establishing on earth among those who believed in him and into which we are called to enter.

Spiritual rebirth

Spiritual rebirth was a major element in Jesus' teaching on entering the Kingdom. We have already referred to his conversation with Nicodemus. Jesus went on to point out to this teacher in Israel the logic of his contention that 'unless a man is born again, he cannot see the kingdom of God'. Stating that 'flesh gives birth to flesh, but the Spirit gives birth to spirit. You should not be surprised at my saying, "You must be born again"' (John 3:3, 6, 7), John saw this teaching as a foundation to the Gospel. He states it clearly in the prologue to his Gospel when dealing with the purpose for which God sent the Christ into the world. 'Yet to all who received him, to those who believed in his name, he gave the right to become children of God — children born not of natural descent, nor of human decision or a husband's will, but born of God' (John 1:12–13). This teaching is developed in the Epistle of John. He links being born of God (that is born of the Spirit and not of flesh), or spiritual rebirth, with belief (I John 5:1). 'Everyone who believes that Jesus is the Christ is born of God.' He goes on to say that when we believe that Jesus is Messiah we have the faith to overcome the world. We have victory over the worldly values that dominate the lives of others. Titus reminds us that 'he saved us through the washing of rebirth and renewal by the Holy Spirit' (Titus 3:5).

When someone is spiritually born again the Holy Spirit is given to enable the new Christian to fulfil this new commitment to Christ. It is no surprise that Jesus told his disciples to wait until the Holy Spirit came upon them — that they would then receive power from on high to do God's will. The change in ordinary men and women when the power of the Holy Spirit comes upon them is evident in those who have repented, believed and been born again.

Thus, if we are to gain a clear biblical perspective on what we have come to regard as 'conversion', we must take account of the three major elements in Jesus' teachings that are fundamental to the New Testament. These three elements of repentance, belief and spiritual rebirth are for each individual the prerequisites for 'entering the Kingdom' — hence the title of this book.

Conversion worldwide

The Church worldwide is growing at a faster rate today than at any time since the days of the New Testament Church, much of it in countries hitherto untouched by the gospel. It is not only the *rate* of growth that shows some similarity to the early days of the Christian Era, but also the social circumstances of many of the areas of most rapid growth today. It was said of the Early Church that the blood of the martyrs was the seed of the church. That is still true today. It was said of Jesus that 'the common people heard him gladly' and that the Church of the first three centuries attracted mainly the poor and low in social status. Paul reminded the Corinthian Christians that 'Not many of you were wise by human standards; not many were influential; not many were of noble birth' (I Cor 1:26).

In those parts of the world where evangelism is showing the greatest success today, Paul's words would certainly be true. It is in many of the poorest lands, which we know as the Third World, that multitudes are receiving Christ. These lands are experiencing spiritual awakening as many thousands daily turn to Christ from other faiths and tribal practices. In a number of these countries, especially in South-East Asia, Communist or Islamic governments hostile to Christianity are persecuting Christians.

We rejoice when we see the growth of the Church worldwide, particularly when we see it grow under persecution. The vigour and vitality of new converts in their faith and the totality of their commitment are reminders to us in the West of past eras of faithful men and women. They are also a necessary reminder that God's ways are not man's ways and that he does still 'work in mysterious ways his wonders to perform'. We in the West do not have, and could never have, a complete theological understanding — we see only in part, as Paul reminds us: 'Now we see but a poor reflection as in a mirror; then we shall see face to face' (I Cor 13:12).

In the countries now experiencing spiritual awakening, there are many indications of a fresh revelation of God's nature and purposes. If we are willing to learn from our brothers and sisters in Christ who live in nations with cultures very different from the Western world, we can receive not only an enrichment to our spiritual experience through their faith and confidence in Christ, but also an increase in our understanding of God.

There has been a tendency, particularly among Europeans, to believe in a Western monopoly of biblical scholarship and to view with suspicion any deviation from Western experience and interpretation. This has been especially true of the popular modern evangelical view of conversion, which centres on a one-off experience that must be expressed in 'acceptable' terms to be counted valid. This has become a legalistic test of faith, a test of righteousness, and a test of theological soundness.

The fallacy of such a narrow concept of conversion is that it can leave our worldly values untouched. It enables us to get on with the business of living in the world, enjoying a materialistic lifestyle and competing in worldly values in the same way as non-Christians, while at the same time actually believing that we are righteous because of that once-in-a-lifetime experience. We convince ourselves that God actually sanctifies, blesses and condones our materialistic acquisitiveness.

We see this carried to extremes in the modern 'prosperity' teaching that has emanated from some American evangelical churches. The teaching that coined the phrase 'God wants you rich' is having an impact upon many Christians in Europe at this time — although it is the very opposite of Jesus' teaching about the Kingdom. Nowhere did Jesus say 'God wants you rich'. He said, 'Blessed are you who are poor, for yours is the kingdom of God' (Luke 6:20).

Kingdom values

Such a total reversal of the kingdom values of Jesus' teaching that are propagated by some of the more extreme modern prosperity cults stems from a defective view of conversion. It is because 'conversion' rather than the fuller biblical concept of 'entering the Kingdom' has become the norm of the modern church in the West that such a travesty and betrayal of the teaching of Jesus could result.

Jesus' teaching on riches is abundantly clear: 'Do not store up for yourselves treasures on earth, where moth and rust destroy, and where thieves break in and steal. But store up for yourselves treasures in heaven, where moth and rust do not destroy, and where thieves do not break in and steal' (Matt 6:19–20). 'It is hard for a rich man to enter the kingdom of heaven' (Matt 19:23).

Clear, too, is Jesus' teaching on other kingdom values: on humility he taught, 'Be careful not to do your "acts of righteousness" before men, to be seen by them. If you do, you will have no reward from your Father in heaven' (Matt 6:1); and 'For everyone who exalts himself will be humbled, and he who humbles himself will be exalted' (Luke 14:11); 'I tell you the truth, unless you change and become like little children, you will never enter the kingdom of heaven (Matt 18:3); and 'Whoever wants to become great among you must be your servant' (Mark 10:43).

On vengeance he taught, 'You have heard that it was said, "Eye for eye, and tooth for tooth." But I tell you, Do not resist an evil person. If someone strikes you on the right cheek, turn to him the other also' (Matt 5:38–39).

On aggression he taught, 'You have heard that it was said, "Love your neighbour and hate your enemy." But I tell you: Love your enemies and pray for those who persecute you, that you may be sons of your Father in heaven' (Matt 5:43–45).

On love he taught, '"Love the Lord your God with all your heart and with all your soul and with all your mind." This is the first and greatest commandment. And the second is like it: "Love your neighbour as yourself." All the Law and the Prophets hang on these two commandments' (Matt 22:37–40).

Finally, Jesus' teaching on the contrast between worldly values and kingdom values is summed up in the phrase, 'For whoever wants to save his life will lose it, but whoever loses his life for me will find it' (Matt 16:25).

These are the kingdom values. They are far away from the values of some of the so-called 'born-again movements' in Europe and America, which have been based on an inadequate view of conversion, and therefore on defective biblical teaching.

Christians in the Western churches today urgently need to take a fresh look at the whole subject of entering the Kingdom from the standpoint of New Testament teaching, and to see its relevance to our present situation.

Secular Europe

Europe today is probably the most highly secularised society in world history yet the most remarkable fact of the present situation is that the secularism of today developed out of the Christian ethos of the past. Europe was once the Christian centre of the world. It produced the Reformation, enormous advances in biblical scholarship, and the modern missionary movement that has carried the gospel around the world. The heart of European Christianity — but ironically also Europe's downfall — lay in its intellectualisation of the gospel and its pride in biblical scholarship. The relentless 'pursuit of the truth' eventually led to the denial of all truth. The nineteenth-century Enlightenment not only produced great intellectual theologians but also a scientific atheism that challenged the foundations of belief and gradually eroded faith in God, the simplicity of trust, and the reality of spiritual experience.

Thus Europe today is a post-Christian society in which many of the values of the Kingdom that laid the foundations of social order have been lost or distorted by generations of unbelief and the onslaught of social Darwinism and Marxist dialectic materialism. Despite the secularism of the age there is a vast amount of superstition, occultism, and belief in a multitude of false religions. When men cease to believe in God they do not believe nothing: they believe anything! Hence when the gospel is faithfully proclaimed today to modern Europeans, it needs to be preached with the same emphasis that Jesus used in his ministry. 'The time has come! The kingdom of God is at hand! Repent! Believe! Be spiritually reborn!'

We still need that call for radical change — a repentance from past false beliefs and from commitment to wrong lifestyles — a total turning away from the secular world and a turning towards God. The power for such a turning can come only from God through spiritual rebirth.

Moral America

If the gospel has been secularised in Europe, in America it has been moralised. The epitome of this process is to be seen in the Moral Majority Movement, which has largely equated moral values and actions with belief in Christ and spiritual rebirth. Jesus condemned the legal moralists of his day — the Pharisees — in the same way that John the Baptist had before him. The Pharisees failed to learn that their strict observance of the Law, their good works and clean living did not bring salvation. That message, at the heart of the gospel, still needs to be heard today.

Europe and America are the two richest continents in the world. Jesus' comment to his disciples following his conversation with the rich young man is particularly relevant with its warnings of the difficulties the rich will encounter when attempting to enter the Kingdom. 'I tell you the truth, it is hard for a rich man to enter the kingdom of heaven. Again I tell you, it is easier for a camel to go through the eye of a needle than for a rich man to enter the kingdom of God' (Matt 19:23–24). This may be interpreted as a warning to the rich nations of the West, that the poorer nations of the Third World will enter the Kingdom first.

Signs of hope

But there are hopeful signs, particularly in Britain where the loss of Empire, economic power and military might have caused a radical rethinking of the national status. Gone is the nationalistic jingoism of the past that produced a belief in the ability of people to solve all problems and overcome all obstacles in their own might. Most importantly, gone is the concept that to be English is to be Christian. Increasingly, people recognise that we are not born Christian but must be born again, and that this spiritual rebirth comes through a personal decision to accept Christ.

Paradoxically, perhaps, the most hopeful signs in Britain are the humbling of the nation; its fall from past glories; and even the loss of influence, power and status of the Church. There are many indications that churches are rediscovering their biblical *raison d'être* and giving evangelism priority at a time when the loss of national self-confidence is producing conditions that make for a fruitful response to the gospel. This is clearly demonstrated as thousands of young people turn to Christ every year and by the fact that the largest student organisations throughout the colleges and universities of Britain are Christian.

The British experience underlines the teaching of Jesus in placing the call to repentance at the very beginning of his announcement of the Good News. *Metanoia* — repentance and turning — is the prerequisite of a fresh outpouring of the Spirit of God upon a nation. This is the subject of this book. Each chapter examines a different aspect of conversion or entering the Kingdom. These contributions could have great significance for the future of the churches in the Western world if we are faithfully to preach the full message of Christ in days of mounting world tension and crisis, and if the Church is to carry out its mission of leading people away from a confidence in human endeavour to a fresh trust and confidence in God and his good purposes for humankind.

Notes

1 Hampole, *Psalter*, xvii, 53 (c 1340). 'In conversyon of synful men.'
2 Thomas à Kempis, *Imitation of Christ*, I, xiii (c 1430). 'Some men have most grevus temptacious in the begynnyng of her (their) conversion, somme in the ende ...'; also John Milton, *Paradise Lost*, XI, 724 (1667). 'And to them preached conversion and repentance'; also John Wesley, *Works*, I, 279 (1740). '... the very beginning of your conversion to God'.
3 Definitions from *Analytical Greek Lexicon* (Samuel Bagster).
4 A J Krailsheimer, *Conversion* (SCM Press: London, 1980), p 6.

2
a biblical perspective

GEORGE CAREY

*Dr George Carey has been Principal of Trinity College, Bristol, since 1982.
He was formerly Vicar of St Nicholas's Church, Durham, about which he
wrote the book* The Church in the Market Place. *His other books include*
I Believe in Man *and* The Gate of Glory.

*He continues our study of the subject of conversion by looking at the
confusion caused by the word in different sectors of the Church. He then
takes us back to look at the use of the terms* metanoia, epistrepho *and*
anagennan *to help us understand the biblical teaching on the subject. He
concludes by looking at some of the applications of conversion in our modern society — conversion and baptism, conversion and ecumenism, and
conversion and society.*

What do the following people have in common — St Paul, St Augustine,
Thomas Aquinas, Martin Luther, Malcolm Muggeridge, Mother Teresa and
Billy Graham? Not a lot, we might think. But they do share one significant
thing. All of them took a decisive step towards Jesus Christ — a step that
marked out their discipleship and allegiance to him. Each of them, in different ways and with different needs, said 'yes' to his call to follow.

This 'turning', this 'yes', this 'following' we call conversion.[1] This word
is a technical term for a cluster of concepts in the Bible which speak of a
person or nation's response to God or his claims upon us through Jesus
Christ. But first we have to note the extreme confusion that rages around
the word and the ideas which gave it its birth. Not everyone agrees that it
is a useful or necessary category to use of the Christian life. For some,

especially within the Catholic tradition, the notion of 'conversion' with its image of a decisive break and certain knowledge of a meeting with God, appears to clash with the emphasis upon the sacramental and the concept of the Christian life as a smooth uphill journey with no sudden sharp twists and turns. There does not appear to be any need of a theology of conversion if from baptism to the last rites — from cradle to grave — God's grace is known and God's grace is given. In contrast with the Reformers, the Council of Trent viewed the idea of assurance of salvation as an arrogant and subjective notion. 'No one can know with the certainty of faith,' it declared, 'that he has obtained the grace of God.'[2]

With the rise of liberalism, liberals — anxious to show that God's grace is equally at work and as valid in the world as in the Church — find the notion of conversion embarrassing, as daring to suggest that some people might be unconverted; they see it as an unwarranted slur upon the effectiveness of God's love and grace. Within liberalism, then, the emphasis falls upon all of mankind being within the circumference of God's grace. Those who are not Christians do not lack his grace — only the eyes to see him. Thus the task of the Church becomes largely a matter of education.

Against these two models of the Christian life, the evangelical way with its emphasis upon conversion and regeneration may seem to be much closer to the pattern we observe in the New Testament and the Early Church. This I shall certainly contend, but not at the expense of truth I observe within the other traditions. The Reformers were certainly right to place stress upon the individual turning to God, arguing that far from being an arrogant notion dependent upon subjective feelings, assurance of salvation is grounded in the promises of God. If he declares we are saved, then we are saved — and that's that.

But the evangelical pattern is not without its problems and weaknesses. Let me cite two. First, the evangelical understanding of conversion can lead to a pietistic and individualistic understanding of the Christian life with a consequent ignoring of the importance and necessity of the Church. 'God has spoken to *me*: *I* have been converted.' It is hardly surprising, therefore, that one of evangelicalism's most constant problems is the tension between corporate and the individual expressions of faith.

The second problem is that evangelicalism has separated conversion from its sacramental roots. There are reasons for this which, to be sure, were not caused by evangelicals, but we have to acknowledge some responsibility for the severing of the close ties between conversion and baptism, between the outward and the inward, and between sacrament and faith. It is hardly surprising, therefore, that many young Christians, baptised as infants but coming to a mature faith in Christ in later life, often in the context of an intense and emotional conversion, feel the psychological need for a sacramental expression of it. They are not convinced by our argument that they were soundly and validly baptised as infants and that there is nothing to do. 'You tell us' they respond, 'that baptism is the sacrament of initiation, of conversion. You tell us of its theological importance in the New Testament and its centrality in the life of the Early Church. And now you cheat us of sharing in its joy because our experience has just caught up with *your* theology.' I have the greatest of sympathy with those who feel the need for that sacramental expression, even though I think they are mistaken when they cry to be re-baptised.

As you will observe then, the issues are far from academic. Indeed, I could add another sobering point to emphasise the need for the Church at large to clarify its theology of conversion and initiation — that is, the churches and fellowships which are growing are those which have a clear doctrine of conversion and are not afraid to make this a central plank in their preaching. So we need to ask again: What is the biblical doctrine of conversion and what are its implications for us today?

The biblical teaching about new life in Christ

There are three important word roots at the heart of a doctrine of conversion: 'to repent', 'to turn' and 'to be born again'. There are, of course, many others which bear upon the theme, such as 'to believe' and 'to confess', but for the sake of clarity we will tackle these three more important words only.

Change of direction (metanoia)

Our word 'repent' is a poor and unsatisfactory translation of the word *metanoia* which means a lot more than 'to be sorry'. *Meta-noia*, as the word suggests, means 'to think again', 'to have second thoughts' and hence, by implication — 'to change direction'. When John the Baptist came preaching *metanoia* he called people to turn from the old life of selfishness and sin to a new life of righteousness which befitted the kingdom of God. When Jesus followed this by preaching the Kingdom and calling on people to 'repent (*metanoia*) and believe the good news' (Mark 1:15), we can see the twofold nature of conversion in its negative and positive aspects. The negative demand is the unconditional turning away from the old life. There is a mental change of direction — a change of purpose and intention — away from the former things and there is a turning towards a new centre of reference which is Jesus Christ himself. The positive aspect is, of course, Jesus himself. 'Repent and believe the good news' — Good News in which he is the central factor.

Naturally, then, *metanoia* became a central element in the early preaching. The first sermon recorded in Acts ends with the appeal to '*Repent* and be baptised, every one of you, in the name of Jesus Christ, so that your sins may be forgiven. And you will receive the gift of the Holy Spirit' (Acts 2:38). The word is so frequent that it is not necessary to hammer the point I am making. It occurs in the accounts of the apostles' preaching in chapters 3, 4, 5, 8, 11 and 13 and so on, and shows the decisive nature of allegiance to Jesus Christ. Indeed, we can point to three important elements within this aspect of conversion.

First, God's call to *metanoia* is a reminder of the moral character of the gospel and the new life which issues from it. There cannot be a gospel without there first being law. So P T Forsyth appealed to preachers of his day: 'For God's sake do not tell poor prodigals ... they are better than they think, that they have more of Christ in them than they know, and so on.' Forsyth saw the need to preach a gospel of salvation which was in real rapport with deep guilt and redemption with holy judgement.[3]

Second, conversion for the early Christians was a message of joy because of the new relationship which came about by turning to God. The three parables told by Jesus and recorded in Luke 15 express in three different ways the joy in heaven and God's gladness when sinners turn to him. 'There is more rejoicing in heaven over one sinner who repents than over ninety-nine righteous persons who do not need to repent' (15:7).

Third, like faith, *metanoia* is not something which is confined to the beginning of the Christian life. The Christian is called to a lifelong *metanoia*. The bias of sin in our lives — even in the lives of those who have found him as Saviour and Lord — is such that we live continually under the Cross and must go to it constantly for forgiveness and renewal.

Turning to God (epistrepho)

We pass now from *metanoia* with its meaning of change of mind or heart to that of actual, physical turning. The verb *epistrepho* only occurs 36 times in the New Testament but is used in the Greek translations of the Old Testament to translate a commonplace Old Testament verb root, *shub*. Within the Old Testament Scriptures it often conveys the ordinary meaning of 'turning' towards something or someone. But it also is often used to convey a religious and moral meaning as, for example, in Jeremiah 11:10 where the people of Judah are accused of turning away from Yahweh and towards evil.

Of those 36 occurrences of 'turning', half are used of turning to God and have a theological meaning of 'conversion'. For example, Paul in II Corinthians 3:16 speaks of the 'veil' of unbelief being removed when a man turns to the Lord. But the most graphic and interesting usages of *epistrepho* occur in the Acts of the Apostles where it expresses the experience of those turning from darkness to light, from one order of existence to another. In Acts 14:15 Paul preaches the Good News that his hearers should turn from 'worthless things [ie, false gods] to the living God'. In chapter 15 the radical meaning of turning to the living God is continued. Paul and Barnabas report 'how the Gentiles had been converted' (15:3), and we see from verses 7–10 that the elements of the conversion are described in terms of 'hearing' the gospel and 'believing' and having 'faith'. Many of these terms come together again in 26:17–18 where the commission to the apostles is described as opening the eyes of the blind to 'turn them from darkness to light, and from the power of Satan to God, so that they may receive forgiveness of sins'.

Two verses later Paul combines *metanoia* with *epistrepho* — 'that they should repent and turn to God'. The twofold content of conversion becomes very plain in that verse; the convert turns 'away' from the old life and turns 'to' God.

New life (anagennan)

It would appear that each of the New Testament writers had his favourite expression for the cataclysmic experience of new life in Christ. For the synoptic writers it is understood, as we have seen, in terms of 'repentance' and 'entering the Kingdom'; for the writer of Acts it is the twin concepts of 'repentance' and 'turning to' God; for Paul we might say that 'justification by faith' and sonship become the central categories. But for the fourth Gospel the word which holds the stage is that of 'new birth'. This is John's favourite metaphor and it is clear that the chief idea is that through believing in Christ, people who were without God now have his life in them so that they become new people.

The background to this very important idea in the Old Testament has its roots in Ezekiel, Jeremiah and Joel. These prophets foresaw the day of the Messiah coming when there would be such a renewal of God's Spirit that he would inhabit the hearts and minds of individuals. To some degree the vision arose from prophetic despair; time and again, God had called upon his people to repent but the response had been wilful defiance. Such was the power of sin that it became obvious that if renewal were to be a reality it had to come from God.

The word 'regeneration' only occurs twice in the New Testament. The first reference, Matthew 19:27–28, refers to the renewal of all things and to this idea we shall return later. The second reference, Titus 3:5, refers to the rebirth of the individual and is more directly in line with the rich seam of 'new birth' images we find in the New Testament, especially in the Johannine writings. Within the Johannine corpus being 'born anew' or 'born from above' is a familiar idiom (John 1:13; 3:5, 6, 8; I John 2:29; 3:9, 4:7; 5:1, 4, 18). John 3 is a very familiar passage to us all and expresses the point that by nature we cannot 'see' the kingdom of God. We need a new nature to enter it. Jesus there explains that our present existence, which is described as *sarx* (sinful flesh), is so shot through with alienation that nothing less than a total renewal of the whole person will do. That new life is brought about by the work of the Spirit who breathes into the Christian life, invading and transforming it.

But the imagery of new birth is not confined to the Johannine literature. We find it, for example, in I Peter. The opening verses throb with the joy of experiencing the transforming power of the new life. 'Praise be to the God and Father of our Lord Jesus Christ! In his great mercy he has given us new birth into a living hope through the resurrection of Jesus Christ from the dead' (1:3). It is possible that such words as 'hope' and 'resurrection' linked with 'new birth' may suggest that the writer has baptism in mind but we cannot be sure of that. A little later, Peter states: 'You have been born again (*anagegennemenoi*), not of perishable seed, but of imperishable, through the living and enduring word of God' (1:23).

At this point it is helpful to ask: To what is regeneration anchored? That is, what is its root? There would appear to be two elements which give the 'new birth' motif its objective character. The first is the historic deeds of Jesus Christ in living, dying and rising for us. We saw this plainly enough in the first verse cited from I Peter. The modern church would do well to take this to heart. The Resurrection, particularly, is seen in the New Testament as the bedrock of Christian initiation and experience. We know from C H Dodd's important book *The Apostolic Preaching and its Development*[4] that a sixfold shape emerged very early in the primitive preaching in which the life, death and resurrection of Jesus was the cornerstone of the proclamation. In essence, as Dodd makes clear, the first preachers stressed that Jesus Christ is Lord; in him God is making all things new; turn to him for salvation.

The second anchorage point lies in the rite of baptism. Titus 3:3–7 speaks of the saving act of God, 'through the washing of rebirth and renewal by the Holy Spirit, whom he poured out on us generously through Jesus Christ our Saviour'. Most expositors believe that baptism is in view here and such a verse shows that the first Christians saw no tension between the inner and the outward. But even though the washing refers to baptism, it has a deeper washing in mind as well, namely the inner cleansing of soul and spirit through the application of the Cross by the Holy Spirit. We shall be touching upon the issue of conversion and baptism a little later but for a moment I would ask you to consider this question also: Why do we consider baptism to be an unrepeatable rite? Why are all the denominations firm on this point? We saw earlier that a strong case may be made out for a perpetual *metanoia* in the life of the believer. Why should there not, then, be many washings, many baptisms for sin? Would it not make more sense to follow the discipline of the Essenes at Qumran and have frequent baptismal washings? The finality of baptism has nothing to do with the rite as such but rather with the meaning of regeneration. There can only be one beginning to the Christian life. If you turn to Christ and his Spirit in you has made you a new creation, then this is unrepeatable. Baptism, therefore, records this epoch-making event in the life of the new Christian. In other words, it is not the rite of baptism which is unrepeatable, as such, but the new birth which it enshrines, and, in so far as it does this, we deem that the rite itself should not be repeated.

I said earlier that the 'rebirth' image was not familiar in Paul's Letters but for the sake of completeness I should acknowledge that the idea is certainly present in his thought. He speaks of a Christian being a 'new creation' (II Cor 5:14ff) and in his teaching about the Christian life draws attention to the work of the Spirit through whom we are 'born' (Gal 4:29) and through whom the fruits of the Spirit come (Gal 5:22f). His slave/child contrast in Romans 8 depends for its validity upon the idea that we now have a new nature and can cry 'Abba, Father' (Rom 8:15).

There can be little doubt then that the concept of rebirth or regeneration is a powerful image which represented a number of different things to the first Christians. First, it represented the start of a new relationship with God; indeed, it denoted God's work. It was a gift. Second, it denoted the saving and renewing of the person through the work of Jesus Christ and through the ministry of the Spirit. Third, it emerged in a transformed life. There could be no denying the authenticity of the life of the 'born again' Christian. Hence Paul's emphasis upon putting off the 'old nature' and 'putting on' Christ. In these days when we shift uncomfortably when our secular press carries front-page articles on 'born again' Christians, we do well to pause and consider why we should not be proud to acknowledge that we have been anew by the Spirit of God.

Regeneration and conversion

Perhaps now we can consider the question: Is there any difference between regeneration and conversion? I think there is, not so much in the nature they embody as the different aspects they represent. Conversion is the work of God but it also describes our work as well. We can turn; we can turn away as well as turn to God and the appeal of evangelistic preaching must be to work upon man's intellect and will, to help and to urge: 'Be reconciled to God.' It would appear, then, that to some degree conversion is something we contribute towards, but not so regeneration. The New Birth is God's work from beginning to end. We can say with Jesus 'You must be born again' but it can never be a command as 'repent' and 'turn' can be. Another distinction I offer concerns the time element in the conversion/regeneration cycle. Conversion suggests a completed act. 'So and so is a converted man.' But regeneration may suggest a process which passes into the completed act. The Spirit's work in leading people to New Birth can continue over months and years. Indeed, we may understand that controversial phrase in the baptism service concerning infants: 'Seeing this child is now regenerate' in that light. The work of God has begun. The Russian scholar Stanislaw Lec once observed in a memorable phrase: 'God never leaves identical fingerprints.' That is, when his Spirit works in a person he will always work according to our needs and distinctive personality. That sensitive touch by the Spirit gives infinite permutations of the ways people experience the 'New Birth'. Some suddenly, some slowly; some with noise and thunder, others with stealth and quiet. All different, but all touched by the same Spirit. But however long or short the process may be it always passes through a fundamental barrier which becomes clearly visible even if we cannot point to the time when we were born spiritually. As C H Spurgeon so graphically remarked years ago, 'A person doesn't need to know the date of his birth to know that he is alive', so what matters to God and us is not a conversion date but that we are truly alive!

We have seen, then, in this study of conversion that it is not on the periphery of New Testament teaching but at its very heart and fundamental to the Christian life. How oddly this emphasis clashes with academic theology and ecclesial practice! It is striking how very few books and articles have been written on this most crucial of themes. I was amazed to find in the preparation of this chapter that Vincent Taylor's splendid book *Forgiveness and Reconciliation* does not even have a section on conversion and regeneration and this goes for the majority of books which explore relevant themes like baptism, reconciliation, forgiveness and so on. Yet when a theology of conversion is ignored we stand in danger of getting the rest of our theology out of perspective. Let me now go on to outline three major areas where a balanced, biblical theology of conversion needs to come into contact with other dimensions of Christian living.

Implications today

Conversion and baptism

It is one of the great ironies as well as tragedies that Catholics and evangelicals have torn conversion and baptism asunder, each holding tenaciously to one half of biblical truth. The New Testament does not know of faith which was not expressed sacramentally, neither does it know of a sacrament which does not proceed from faith. So Michael Schmaus, the well-known Roman Catholic theologian argues: 'Paul knows no baptism that is not born of faith and nourished by it; so also he recognizes no faith that does not realize itself in the sacrament.'[5] In the New Testament period a Christian unattached to a church would have been an incomprehensible notion since a person's new birth into God's family expressed in the baptismal rite led him into the fellowship of the local church, which was the local manifestation of the kingdom of God of which he was now an heir.

The link between conversion and baptism is clearly seen in the earliest known rites of baptism. In one of the earliest, given to us by Justin Martyr in the second century, baptism is described as 'the washing of regeneration' and in subsequent accounts of baptism conversion is vividly expressed in the turning away from the Devil to the Lord. Fourth-century rites describe this most graphically. At the section 'The Renouncing of the Devil', questions are asked of the candidate. The candidate turns symbolically to the West, the direction of darkness because it is the place where the sun goes down, and says 'I renounce thee, Devil, and all thy works.' He then turns to the East and cries with joy: 'I believe and bow before thee, Father, Son and Holy Spirit.' Symbolically there was expressed the fact that the baptised person passed from the dominion of darkness to the kingdom of Christ.[6]

In certain sections of the Church another custom was added which became popular. After turning to the West and renouncing Satan the candidate was expected to expectorate forcibly before turning to the East. This spitting at Satan was a robust symbol of hostility to the Devil and all his works and demonstrated the Church's belief in the step of faith which had been taken by the new Christian. We can understand then why conversion and baptism were seen by the first Christians as a unity and why the 'sealing' of the Holy Spirit (Eph 1:13) could be used quite naturally of the act of baptism itself. Thus in the Early Church to the question 'When did you become a Christian, or a member of the Church?' the most natural answer would have been 'I was baptised on such-and-such a date.'

I have already drawn attention earlier to the problems that a theology of conversion causes when it is divorced from its sacramental context and I suggest that we need to discover ways of contextualising conversion within a sacramental framework. The increasing secularisation of our society suggests that the majority of converts in the days to come will be those who have not been baptised as infants and the most natural context for them to express their new-found faith is in the symbolism of baptism. It may not be too long before evangelists making their appeal invite unbaptised people who have just accepted Christ to step into the waters of baptism. But I feel just as strongly that those who *have* been baptised as infants and who in later years have made a decision for Christ should be allowed, and should be expected, to make some form of declaration which is public. If by 'sacramental' we mean 'that outward form in which God's grace comes and authenticates the inner response of faith' the sacramental channel may be a testimony given by a new convert followed by the laying on of hands; the Reaffirmation of Baptismal Vows or some other conceivable public act.[7]

But it is also very important for us to develop and strengthen the other aspect of this, namely, the rite of baptism. The Early Church was not afraid to put up its fences here. And yet, as Harnack notes in his major work on the spread of the Church, evangelism seemed to go hand in hand with a rigorous attitude to the sacrament of baptism.[8] On the one hand, it was characteristic of Christianity that every serious believer saw himself as a witness and herald. The gospel was preached freely. On the other hand, the Church built walls and barriers around itself. It appeared to offer its life grudgingly. But this was only because it wanted to be sure that believers knew what it was all about. Careful teaching was required before catechumens were baptised. They were taught the Scriptures, they were shown the mysteries of their deliverance from evil, and they were taught to pray. Finally the great day came when they too entered the waters of baptism and so symbolically passed from death to life.

I seem to be saying two contradictory things. How can we set up evangelistic structures which call upon people to respond in baptism and yet set up baptismal structures which demand careful thought, thorough preparation and teaching? The tension, of course, was there in the days of the New Testament and the Early Church, but I suggest the answer may lie in the difference between the evangelistic moment and pastoral ministry. In *pastoral ministry* we need to rediscover the role of baptismal teaching and discipline — and I would remind you that this is the order we find in the Early Church — teaching then discipline. We must urge the contemporary church to make much more of the possibilities for growth in baptismal initiation and Christian nurture. Let us make as much as possible of the high points of the Christian year, perhaps even restoring Easter as the time for baptisms. In *evangelistic preaching* we should be more conscious of the need for what I have called 'sacramental expression' and seek to find ways of people nailing their colours to the mast.

Conversion and ecumenism

I pointed out earlier the vivid contrast between Catholic and evangelical modes of understanding the beginning of the Christian life. For the Catholic, the Church is often seen as a great sacramental reality into which we enter and through which God's grace comes to nourish. For the evangelical, a chasm exists between sinful man and a holy God, and conversion to him through 'believing', 'repenting' and 'accepting' is the way into life. It seems that we have here two completely different ways of finding Christ's salvation.

I do not think that need be the case. In these days, faced with the enormous task of a world in need of the message of God's love and grace, we cannot afford to indulge in polemics or to write one another off. The involvement of Roman Catholics in Mission England indicates that they did not see the message of conversion as a contradiction of their theology of the Church but, rather, as something which harmonises with it. Let me offer a number of reflections in the ecumenical significance of conversion.

First, a true theology of conversion emphasises the importance of

Jesus. Catholics at the time of the Reformation shied away from a theology which seemed to exaggerate individual assurance. But, properly speaking, conversion is confrontation with Jesus Christ, standing before him in need of his love and grace. It is our positive verdict when confronted by his life, values and standards; we make our commitment to follow.

Second, if evangelicals are deficient in separating conversion from baptism, it must surely be admitted that Catholics are often guilty of holding on to the rite of baptism and letting go of conversion. We need to be asking of Catholic and non-evangelical churches today: What are you calling people from and to? Don't be surprised to find that if you sow no seed you get no growth. Churches which see the Church as a sacrament of grace — and I see nothing basically wrong in this idea — must work out for themselves a rational link between baptism and conversion which will be a real calling of sinners to a Saviour, and a real turning from darkness to light.

The social implications of conversion

Our main attention in this chapter has been upon the conversion of the individual and his relationship to God. But I must now develop a hint I dropped earlier, that conversion affects the whole of creation. This, I said, was the thrust of Matthew 19:28. And I believe it is vitally important for us to understand that New Testament teaching concerning individuals turning to Christ has its place within a theology of God's relationship with the whole of creation which has radical implications for everything. Jesus preached the coming of God's kingdom; the early preachers expected Jesus to return in power and glory and, accordingly, preached repentance and faith with urgency and conviction; St Paul himself looked forward, not only to the redemption of the individual, but to the redemption and renewal of all things (Rom 8:18f). I could go on to show that the Scriptures never separated eschatology from the doctrine of salvation.

It is important, then, to absorb the fact that conversion in the New Testament means that everything in creation will one day return to the lordship of Christ. The simple confession 'Jesus is Lord', probably a baptismal confession, was in itself a profound statement of the radical consequences of taking upon one his lordship. Not only did it lead to a changed life, affecting one inwardly, but it had important implications concerning the attitude of the believer to life itself and to his society in particular. It meant that one's moral standards were governed by those of Jesus Christ — he came first and everything else ran a poor second. Christians were not afraid to risk all for him and many suffered the most terrible of punishments for their stubbornness in putting Christ's standards before all else.

The character of conversion in the early days of Christianity stands in great contrast to the insipid, pietistic version of the modern Western church. We have too sharply individualised it and, thereby, tamed it. Consequently, our theology and experience of conversion scarcely compares favourably with its vigorous, radical and full-blooded counterpart in Scripture. We have only to ask these questions to see how we have chained it up. Does the Church's theology of conversion include within it an expectation and earnest desire which embraces the transformation of all things? What, indeed, are the political implications of conversion? We have to confess that most Western Christians haven't even *begun* to grapple with such issues.

Similarly, when we turn to the implications of being Christians in a society in need of God we become aware when we read the Bible that we do not 'live conversion' as the first Christians did. What have we left to follow Christ? Houses, land, jobs, bright prospects and families? We shift uneasily when we hear of such 'turnings' and by cunning exegesis persuade ourselves that it is different these days.

All right, let us try another approach. We live in a world with great problems — poverty, inequality and injustice. When did we, in our churches, last consider radical reductions in our standard of living so that we might make a greater contribution to the needs of others? When did the Church last take a daring initiative similar to Live Aid? 'But aren't you taking conversion far beyond its meaning?' someone might protest. No, I don't think I am. Conversion is about the difference Christ makes to our lives by claiming us lock, stock and barrel — and too often our version of conversion is so mild that others can't tell the difference between our new life and the old life of others. May I suggest two major shifts that have to be taken in Christian thinking if our notions of conversion are to carry an effective appeal to our age.

First, it will affect the body-life of our churches. New life means that we are born into a new family — the family of the redeemed. Often the quality of church life contradicts our preaching of salvation. 'You Christians will have to look more redeemed before I start believing in your Saviour' the philosopher Nietzsche apparently said. But when Christian fellowships start living the radical life of love which Jesus called us to, they have the capacity to become families which draw others into their love and life.

Second, where Jesus is really acknowledged Lord, the Church's message passes beyond a mere religious appeal to radical social and political questions. If Jesus calls all men to repent and to be 'born again' we cannot live segregated lives but we are all one in Christ Jesus. Hence the stand of the different churches in South Africa, for full incorporation of black people into the South African human family, is but an extension of the theology of conversion. Christ calls us to himself and when we turn and follow, we follow as brothers, sisters and equals. That transforming 'newness' brought about by the Spirit calls the Church to be 'salt' and 'light' in society.

We have studied conversion's biblical roots and noted that its centrality in Scripture clashes strangely with the modern church which has, by and large, relegated it to a minority pursuit. It is surely time we discovered what the New Testament took for granted, that a strong theology of conversion is at the heart of a growing, vibrant Christianity.

Notes

1 Literature on conversion is disappointingly meagre. There are very useful word studies in, for example, G Kittel, *Theological Dictionary of the New Testament* (Eerdmans: Grand Rapids, 1964–76), and C Brown, *Dictionary of New Testament Theology* (Paternoster Press: Exeter, 1975–78). I commend N Burkhardt, *The Biblical Doctrine of Regeneration*, Evangelical Monographs no 2 (Paternoster Press: Exeter, 1978).

2 *The Decrees of the Council of Trent*, Session VI.9.

3 P T Forsyth, *Positive Preaching and the Modern Mind (Independent Press: London, 1949), p 106.*

4 C H Dodd, *The Apostolic Preaching and its Development* (Hodder and Stoughton: London, 1936).

5 M Schmaus, 'Justification and the Last Things', *Dogma*, vol 6 (Steed and Ward, 1977): p 6.

6 See J Jungmann, *The Early Liturgy* (Darton, Longman and Todd: London, 1959), p 80ff; and C Pocknee, *Water and the Spirit* (Darton, Longman and Todd: London, 1967), p 35ff.

7 In this connection I consider J Martos, *Doors to the Sacred* (SCM Press: London, 1981) a very thoughtprovoking examination of sacramentality. Martos concludes, 'But once sacraments are understood for what they are — human creations which function as doors to the sacred — there is no intrinsic reason why new sacramental forms could not be invented to reach the same sacred realities that the old forms once revealed' p 530.

3
an international perspective

ARTHUR GLASSER

It is appropriate that we should follow the biblical look at conversion with a look at the contemporary scene in the world church. Dr Arthur Glasser of Fuller Theological Seminary and the School of World Mission in California has written extensively on missiological subjects and here takes a comprehensive look at the broad canvas of the world church and even at conversion to and from other religions. He recognises the diversity of conversion experiences — often worrying as well as challenging — and helps us to define the differences between the Western missionary perspective and the newer indigenous church perspective. He picks out three particular areas where the world church has much to teach the Western church, particularly in Britain. He presents the case for holistic evangelism and shows the need to move away from nominalism; the need for a new look at the powers and principalities and for a new emphasis on the kingdom of God — present not apocalyptic.

Introduction

Our subject is conversion in the world church — a subject so broad that it staggers the imagination. Who is competent to select relevant details from so large a canvas? My assignment is to address those dimensions of this broad and complicated theme that bear on the evangelistic task in Britain today.

When we think of conversion in the world church, we are pressed to begin with an even larger thesis: namely, that many religions as well as all political movements are characterised by some form of conversion phenomenon. Actually, everyone seems to be getting into the conversion debate these days. Some psychologists see it as an acute form of psychosis or the result of inquisitorial brainwashing techniques. One has only to read anthropologist Arnold van Gennep's *The Rites of Passage* to find him using the term conversion when describing 'circumcision rituals' among Muslims or the 'rite of separation' among Hindus or the 'departure from childhood' of Taoists and Confucianists.[1] Then there is the widely publicised account of Arthur Koestler's conversion to Communism. Among other things this Hungarian Jewish journalist stated:

> By the time I had finished with Feuerback and *State and Revolution*, something had clicked in my brain which shook me like a mental explosion. To say that one had seen the light is a poor description of the mental rapture which only the convert knows. The new light seems to pour from all directions across the skull; the whole universe falls into pattern like the stray pieces of a jigsaw puzzle assembled by magic at one stroke. There is now an answer to every question. Doubts and conflicts are a matter of the tortured past — a past already remote, which one lived in dismal ignorance in the tasteless, colorless world of those who *don't know*. Nothing henceforth can disturb the convert's inner peace and serenity — except the occasional fear of losing faith again, losing thereby what alone makes life worth living, and falling back into the outer darkness, where there is wailing and gnashing of teeth.[2]

The uniqueness of conversion

George Carey's chapter reminds us that Christian conversion represents a phenomenon that — in its biblical sense — is unique. This is because the God who provided the Christian gospel through the death, burial, and resurrection of Jesus Christ is uniquely involved in it by his Holy Spirit. During a conversation between several Hindu university professors in Madras and Emil Brunner, the professors asked him to explain how he could affirm of Jesus Christ that 'in none other is there salvation'. In response he pointed out that the finality of Jesus Christ stemmed from the fact that he and he alone died for the sins of the world. 'Neither Buddha nor Krishna nor Rama died for the sins of mankind.' He then went on to state:

> There is one thing you will not find in Indian religion, or in any religion outside Christianity ... a man who came on earth to

reconcile to God by the sacrifice of his life those who have become separated from God by their guilt and sin.[3]

Not only does Christian conversion involve a sense of personal failure, or self-humbling, a radical change of heart, a sincere seeking of God through Jesus Christ, and a new clarity of knowledge touching God and his ways — more fundamentally, it also represents the reality of God at work, imparting life where there was only death (Eph 2:1ff). It is God who resolves the tragedy of spiritual impotence by bestowing nothing less than a second birth, the opening of blinded eyes and sealed hearts, and the illumination of the mind to perceive things previously regarded as foolishness. People respond to the Good News of Jesus Christ because of God's prior working, drawing them to himself in a strong and overwhelming fashion. Conversion begins with what God has done in Christ and is doing through his Spirit. But inevitably it issues in what individuals do by way of response.

Diversity of conversion experiences

When we attempt to make generalisations about the conversion experience with the worldwide church as our data base, we encounter a massive problem. Whereas many Christians will regard their personal encounter with Jesus Christ as the most significant experience in their lives, its details will probably differ markedly from all other conversion experiences even within a single culture. How much more probable the differences in conversion experiences among Christians in diverse cultures. So then, conversions are not only conditioned by the theological paradox of God's seeking grace and his wide-ranging impulses in the individual heart that prompt the conversion quest, but psychological factors also play their part, for conversions to Christ are often triggered by 'the crisis of adolescent identity or the sense of moral and personal failure and the therapeutic need for acceptance'.[4] And the sociological dimension also will be determinative. Historical and cultural factors often conspire to create situations especially propitious for personal spiritual inquiry, for mass evangelistic activity, and for movements of people Christward.[5] Even so, neither psychology nor sociology can explain fully the convert's awareness of his spiritual and moral transformation, and of his sense of a new and abiding linkage with God through his reception of Jesus Christ and the inworking of the Holy Spirit.

Any study of Christian conversion in the world church should begin with a flat repudiation of the penchant of some evangelicals to stereotype conversion. Vernon Grounds has pointed out that all too often conversion is assumed to be 'a cataclysmic experience, a standardized experience, an observable experience, an instantaneous experience, and always a psychologically integrating and spiritually redeeming experience'.[6] Actually, differences in personality and upbringing keep conversion from being standardised as something instantaneous and cataclysmic. It is not always observable, and whereas it ushers a person into a new order of relationships and possibilities, it does not change the person 'immediately, magically or pervasively'. Furthermore, the Bible does not promise psychic health as the invariable result. Indeed, the recent volume *Conversions* (edited by Hugh T Kerr and John M Mulder)[7] is a timely reminder that we need a great deal more information about the ways in which conversion is actually experienced throughout the world.

Those of us who have participated in ecumenical gatherings involving Christians from church traditions, political loyalties, and cultural enclaves not previously encountered will agree that the experience can be painful as well as exhilarating. We meet those whose conceptions of the basic elements of the Christian faith — so it seems — are so horribly distorted that we cannot but conclude that their national backgrounds have largely shaped their understanding of the gospel. Then, when we begin to participate in the discussions, we are startled at the way our most settled convictions are sharply challenged. We begin to fear whether our own understanding of the biblical faith has not been largely coloured by rational or cultural sentiment. This makes us wonder what the gospel of God really is in its essence, whether it is equally valid for every human being. In the painful arena of public debate we come to a new awareness of the need to test all convictions by the Word of God. For, if on the cognitive level of conversion grave differences exist, what of the experiential level?

The conversion of those nurtured in the Church who later come to personal faith and confession of Jesus Christ as Lord will be far different from that of those whose lives had previously been completely outside the Church in the West or under allegiance to another religious system in the non-Western world. I was a God-fearer as a result of my upbringing and somewhat faithful attendance at a local Presbyterian church. My conversion experience at a student conference involved only a radical reorientation of my relationship to Jesus Christ. It barely touched my lifestyle. Nonetheless, there are lessons for the churches in Great Britain that come from reflecting on phenomena of conversion within the Christian movement worldwide. We affirm this without hesitation, despite the fact that religious pluralism in Western Europe and North America is probably far more complex than in Asia, Africa and Latin America. Grappling with this complexity can be helped by reflecting on things observed in less complex situations elsewhere. To these lessons we now turn.

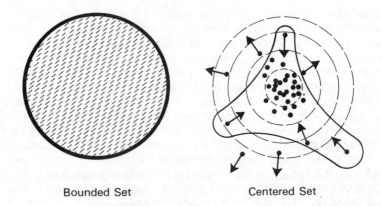

Bounded Set   Centered Set

Western missionary concepts or the centred set perspective

First, however, we must consider the upheavals Western mission-planted churches are currently experiencing throughout the Third World. A shift of significant proportions is taking place. One of my colleagues, Professor Paul G Hiebert, has analysed this in the following fashion.

For many years Western missionaries have tended to look at things in a certain way. Theirs is a 'bounded set' mentality. This means they create a category — called a 'bounded set' — by listing its essential characteristics, and thereby giving it a clear boundary. They then devote considerable effort to defining and maintaining this boundary. This forces them to see all within the set as having uniform and essential characteristics. Furthermore, the set they have established is static and unchanging. Following this line, they define 'Christian' in terms of a set of essential, measurable, definitive characteristics — like right doctrine plus right polity plus right action. According to their definition they know those who are with them — 'sharing our sameness' — and those who are outside — 'not our kind'. True, they recognise that some of their people within the set are better trained and more experienced, whereas some have only just been converted, or have recently transferred in from other denominations. But their major concern is the boundary. They have an 'ecclesiastical' approach to evangelism. It involves getting people to cross their boundary and conform to their category's essential, measurable characteristics. They make this their task worldwide: to multiply themselves. The result is 'mission-planted churches'.

Nowadays many dynamic groups all over the world are coming to see things differently: the thriving independent churches of Asia, Africa, and Latin America, the many 'breakaway' movements that were once part of these static Western 'bounded sets'. They define membership standards loosely — if at all. Their preoccupation is with the centre: lifting up Jesus Christ. They view people in terms of their relation to the centre. Some may be far removed from the centre, but moving towards it. This means that they are within the 'centred set'. Others may be much nearer the centre, but moving away from it. They don't belong. The 'centred set' only consists of those moving towards its centre. The centre is the focus, not the boundary, although the boundary conversion is necessary. Suffice it to say, maintaining the boundary is not as important, provided the centre is kept in clear focus. Hence wide variation is tolerated within the set. The concern is not with uniformity, but with movement towards the centre. Some are far away, coming from one direction; others are much nearer, coming from another direction. Nearness is the dimension of biblical knowledge, spiritual growth and commitment to Jesus Christ, who is the Centre. This mans that the set is dynamic; something is always happening. And this kind of thinking — I'm sure — has already begun to penetrate Great Britain. Indeed, analyse which churches are growing in Britain today. Are they 'bounded set' in mentality, or is their stress on relationship to Jesus Christ, the 'centred set' perspective?

Conversion and holistic evangelism

Despite the current rapid growth of the Christian movement in many parts of the non-Western world, any overall assessment of the present state of the churches is that whereas 'first' and to a lesser degree 'second' generation congregations reflect vitality, the older congregations become increasingly institutionalised, less concerned with personal commitment. For this reason, the evangelisation of any country does not depend on the planting of new congregations so much as the renewal of old ones. Even the emergence of new congregations is no guarantee that they will remain spiritually vital. There is no such thing as a 'steady state' Christian or church. Spiritual life, like all forms of life, is involved in processes of health and illness, of reinvigoration and decay.[8]

When the church is planted in a new community or culture, its 'first generation' members have to pay a high price for their decison to follow Jesus as Lord. They often experience the hostility of family and friends, and know the pain of community ostracism. But they persevere in their profession, and the Spirit of God deepens their relationship to the Lord and to one another within the life and witness of the emerging church.

In contrast, subsequent generations grow up within the framework of the new community without having paid the same price for their faith. Furthermore, their tendency is to draw back from the total commitment that characterised the founding members. Often this results in nominalism — the dominant weakness of the worldwide Christian movement in our

day, particularly in the West, but increasingly in the rest of the world.
Every individual is a reflection of the 'ideas, feelings and values' of his
or her culture. This means that we should recognise the radical nature of
conversion, that it is nothing less than a fundamental change of allegiance:
coming under the lordship of Christ. It does not merely have a cognitive
dimension, that is, understanding and accepting biblical and theological
information regarding God and his redemptive activity in Christ, though
knowledge of the truth is important. Conversion also has an affective
dimension: the gospel confronts us with God himself. The numinous
experience of mystery, awe, and longing, as well as the sense of dread
because of one's moral corruption, must be transformed into the joy of
sins forgiven and conscious participation in Christ in the midst of his
people. However, in the ultimate sense, the gospel deals with values and
allegiances. It is in this evaluative dimension that one acknowledges Christ
as Lord and accepts his righteous rule to the conscious repudiation of all
other loyalties.

Nominalism results when we stop short of allowing the Spirit of God to
penetrate fully all three dimensions of our personality; it results when we
fail to evaluate our world-view, behaviour, and social relationships in the
light of Christ's lordship. Those second and later generation 'Christians'
who grow up in the Church, receive its instruction, and participate in its
sacraments, can all too easily rest content with either the cognitive or
affective dimensions of the gospel (or both!) and yet never get to the point
of giving Christ authority over their lives and values. I once heard a prominent American evangelical, Robert McQuilkin, state that he knew of no
one brought up in a Christian home and church who had made a dynamic
contribution unless he spiritually had first had a crisis experience when he
consciously made Jesus Christ the Lord of his life. All those baptised as
infants or in their youth — often because of parental or peer pressure —
need to realise that baptism only becomes efficacious when the issue of
Christ's lordship is consciously resolved.

So then, we do not tell nominal Christians they are not true believers.
We do not bluntly press conversion on them. Rather, we accept them on
their own terms, meet them as equals, rejoice with them, and share with
them our own spiritual pilgrimage. We seek thereby to gain their trust and
through baptismal language (which may be unfamiliar) and its analogy
with marriage language (which is certainly familiar) help them discover
where they are on the journey of faith. And we constantly keep in mind the
parable of the soils (Luke 8:4–15) with its warning against being content
with a mere cognitive or even an affective grasp of the gospel. The issue
of lordship is only resolved when one 'with a noble and good heart' (8:15)
turns 'from darkness to light, and from the power of Satan to God' (Acts
26:18).

Consider the following illustration from Africa. Aylward Shorter in his perceptive book, *African Christian Theology: Adaptation or Incarnation*, provides us with a telling example we all do well to take to heart.

> During the past hundred years African Traditional Religion has been visibly sinking beneath the surface of modern social life in Africa, but what remains above the surface is, in fact, the tip of an iceberg. At Baptism, the African Christian repudiates remarkably little of his former non-Christian outlook. He may be obliged to turn his back upon certain traditional practices which the Church, rightly or wrongly, had condemned in his area, but he is not asked to recant a religious philosophy. The Church, in any case, takes no cognizance of this philosophy. Consequently, he returns to the forbidden practices as occasion arises with remarkable ease. Conversion to Christianity is for him sheer gain, an 'extra' for which he has opted. It is an overlay on his original religious culture. Apart from the superficial condemnations, Christianity has really had little to say about African Traditional Religion in the way of serious judgements of value. Consequently, the African Christian operates with two thought-systems at once, and both of them are closed to each other. Each is only superficially modified by the other.[9]

This has implications for us all, especially those from traditions that practise infant baptism. We dare not rest content with the vows taken by parents and sponsors when an infant is baptised. If the earlier baptism is to have relevance, the baptised person must later reaffirm the vows personally upon experiencing what Jesus called 'being born again'. Nothing is so crucial as the preparation of young people for confirmation or its equivalent.

Conversion and the 'principalities or powers'

The lordship of Christ extends beyond the individual convert's world-view, values, and relationships. It includes the implications of Christ's exaltation to 'God's right hand — with angels, authorities, and powers in submission to him' (I Peter 3:22). This becomes particularly relevant when we investigate the phenomenon of conversion in the non-Western world. There the issue is one of unmasked power. Conversion involves an encounter between the dominion of darkness and the kingdom of God (Col 1:13). And this encounter is more seriously recognised in areas not deceived by the mechanistic myth of the West which denies the reality of demonic intelligences seeking to discredit Jesus Christ and keep people from coming to faith in him. In Asia, Africa and Latin America

People give their allegiance to Christ when they see that his power is superior to magic and voodoo, the curses and blessings of witch doctors, and the malevolence of evil spirits and that his salvation is a real liberation from the power of evil and death.[10]

Powers in the New Testament

All this brings us back to the New Testament and the concept of world powers that, according to George B Caird 'reaches into every department of Paul's theology so much so that it cannot be dismissed as a survival of primitive superstition' but rather concerns 'spiritual realities with which he and his missionary companions have personal acquaintance'.[11] These powers are created beings, a fact of tremendous significance (Col 1:15–16). They not only owe their very existence to God but were created by Christ, not that they might exist unto themselves in an autonomous fashion, but that they might bring glory to God. They did not stand in opposition to his will, but were positive in their contribution to his creation. Berkhof suggests that they 'served as the invisible weight-bearing substratum of the world ... the linkage between God's love and visible human experience. They held life together, preserving it within God's love, and served as aids to bind men fast in his fellowship; intermediaries not as barriers but as bonds between God and man.[12]

Paul is quite specific about the activity of the powers after that unrevealed event when they 'did not keep their positions of authority but abandoned their own home' (Jude 6; II Peter 2:4). They became 'independent and autonomous, egocentric and self-willed'.[13] We might say that although they retained their God-given power, they began to exercise it as though it were self-achieved. The bent of their natures came to be 'opposition to God' and was expressed by seeking to achieve dominion over the world and over all peoples. They became as gods (Gal 4:8) posing as ultimate realities and intruding between God and his creation. Instead of continuing as the channels of his love, they abruptly became usurpers, seeking the worship that belongs to God alone. In order to achieve this they cast a deluding spirit upon people that caused them to adopt false perspectives on all circumstances and institutions of life, and particularly on all spiritual realities. Through their activity evil is enabled to exist as a force in the world transforming the powers into 'the world rulers of darkness'.[14]

So then, we must regard the powers as 'a roadblock between the Creator and His creation'.[15] Because of their overarching pervasion of all human existence, Paul soberly made the universal declaration that before people come under the liberating lordship of Christ they are following 'the ways of this world and of the ruler of the kingdom of the air, the spirit who is now at work in those who are disobedient' (Eph 2:2). As a result the powers make sure that no society reaches out to God. Berkhof sounds the right note when he states that it should not be difficult for us to perceive today in every realm of life that the powers which unify men, nonetheless separate them from God. He adds:

> The state, politics, class, social struggle, national interest, pub-lic opinion, accepted morality, the ideas of decency, humanity, democracy — these give unity and direction to thousands of lives. Yet precisely by giving unity and direction they separate these many lives from the true God; they let us believe that we have found the meaning of existence, whereas they really estrange us from true meaning.[16]

From the above it will be apparent that despite their fallenness, God uses the powers to enclose people in supportive relationships that function in part in their better interests. Although fallen humans deserve only the judgement of God because of their sin and their desire for an existence separate from him, by means of the powers, God graciously preserves them in reasonably stable societies and cultures. This reality is detailed in Galatians 4:1–11. We would conclude, however, that whereas life apart from Christ can have its good features, Paul regards it as slavery and not to be favourably compared with the liberation that Christ brings.

In the context of describing the redemptive work of Christ, the apostle Paul states that at the cross he 'disarmed the powers and authorities, made a public spectacle of them, triumphing over them by the cross' (Col 2:15). Indeed, 'the reason the Son of God appeared was to destroy the devil's work' (I John 3:8). These texts remind us to go beyond the familiar New Testament thesis that Christ's redemption delivers his people from the guilt of sin. Paul rather speaks of Christ as the One who also liberates his people from their previous slavery and bondage to the powers. Jewish legalism and pagan regulations have lost their power to tyrannise. Social and religious mores which tend to alienate people from God have lost their 'pull' (Col 2:16–23). It is the Crucifixion that proved their undoing.

Furthermore, Jesus Christ was 'declared with power to be the Son of God by his resurrection from the dead' (Rom 1:4). The Resurrection demonstrates the reality of his triumph over the powers themselves. They have been unmasked and stripped of their ultimate weapon — death. Their ancient grip on people has been broken. What remains is merely the capacity for colossal deception. The powers have been 'disarmed' or 'ren-dered ineffective'. Although they will continue to divert people from all preoccupation with God himself, their activity is now devoid of substantial power. All is bluff and illusion. It is as though by the Cross Christ deliber-ately disconnected all the linkages within cultures by which the powers previously held people in bondage. Finally, the powers have become completely powerless when it comes to separating the people of God from his love (Rom 8:38–39).

Powers in the world today

Despite this, their present influence in the world is enormous. They are behind all the pursuit of affluence ('mammon') and the preoccupation with pleasure ('lust' and 'pride'). They entice people to seek solutions to their varied problems through recourse to astrology, necromancy, spiritism, witchcraft — indeed, all forms of the occult. Their devotees can be quite adept at miraculous healings, divination, and speaking in tongues. Satan is indeed the great counterfeiter!

Even so, Christ has won a complete victory over the powers. This fact challenges us not to draw back from the 'power encounter' biblical evangelism demands. In this connection Alan R Tippett has vividly stated:

Sinful man is bound. Christ came to unloose him ... There is no way out in this war, no compromise, no friendly agreement to engage in dialogue, no mere Christian presence ... When we ask ourselves why there had to be an incarnation, a death and a resurrection, we see that there was no other way of overcoming Satan, his works and his authority.[17]

The New Testament and the record of church history bear ample witness to the fact that despite the Cross and the nullification of the powers' real power, their effects still dominate all people to a greater or lesser degree. They relentlessly attack the Church and seek by every means to hinder her missionary obedience. Their abode remains 'in the heavenly realms' surrounding the visible world (Eph 3:10). From there they venture forth to menace, seduce, and in other ways thwart the ongoing movement of the gospel among the nations. Often they do this through incarnating themselves in existing structures in society and in cultural traditions and religious institutions. On occasion, however, they assault individuals directly.

And this brings us to what Paul G Hiebert calls 'the flaw of the excluded middle'.[18] By this he refers to the zone between the seen or empirical world and the presence of God, who fills all things yet is separate from his universe. In this zone are the powers, identifiable in part as the cosmic beings of 'high religions' or as the local beings of 'folk religions'. In the non-Western world the conversion experience is often regarded as the result of gospel proclamation made by those equipped with spiritual gifts to handle the 'power encounter' inescapably involved. In the Western churches the tendency is to regard as obsolete those spiritual gifts mentioned in the New Testament which are not related to the oral ministry of the Word of God. This is because Western Christians tend to accept a mechanistic view of the universe and of the social order that to all practical purposes denies the realities within the middle zone and confines gospel preaching to the cognitive dimension alone. What is forgotten is that 'the kingdom of God is not a matter of talk but of power' (I Cor 4:20). 'It is no coincidence that many of the most successful missions have provided some form of Christian answer to middle level questions'.[19] So long as Western Christians confine God to his supernatural world and regard the natural world as functioning according to autonomous scientific laws, their churches will see little evidence of the sort of life-transforming conversions that characterise much evangelistic outreach in Asia, Africa, and Latin America.

Conversion and the kingdom of God

Evangelicals in our day are becoming increasingly aware of the distortion that comes to their understanding of the gospel when they concentrate on the Gospel of John to the neglect of the Synoptics. This has caused them increasingly to take seriously that which was the dominant theme of Jesus' earthly ministry: the kingdom of God. Earlier generations of evangelicals tended to downplay this theme because of the widely publicised and popularised aberrations of dispensational exegesis (the Kingdom is Israelitish and wholly future) and in reaction to the 'social gospel' of theological liberalism. Howard Snyder, a vigorous evangelical with missionary experience in Brazil, stated in 1983: 'The recent partial recovery among evangelicals of the Kingdom of God theme is surely one of the most significant theological developments of this decade — perhaps of this century.'[20] Since this growing interest is a worldwide phenomenon, we must include it in this discussion because of the contribution it makes to the enlargement of our understanding of conversion.

Some years back there was considerable hostility in the older churches towards the evangelical understanding of conversion. It was dismissed as a pietist heresy, something which allegedly made those who experienced it an encapsulated community preoccupied with their own religious life and indifferent to the appalling needs of the world. In the 60s there were not a few like the prominent theologian who expressed his impatience with this excessive individualism by stating, 'Talk about personal conversion nauseates me'.[21]

But that was almost twenty years ago. No longer do evangelicals attempt the impossible and seek to differentiate 'testifying to the gospel of the grace of God' (for the present church age) from 'preaching the Kingdom' (for a future millennial age). Actually, these are synonymous terms and are found in the same context (Acts 20:24–25). Both refer to the here and now. And yet, the Kingdom is also eschatalogical. For its coming we constantly pray!

So then, evangelicals are beginning to discover that the gospel they are commissioned to preach worldwide is the good news of the kingdom of God. Indeed, they are finding that 'the beginning of the Kingdom through Christ's entry into human history is the main context of conversion in the New Testament.[22] This means that the goal of conversion is not the saving of souls apart from history but that through individuals he is converting, his purpose for the world is being realised. Today, the Christian vision must be enlarged from getting people converted and into the Church that they may get other people converted and into the Church and so *ad infinitum*. By putting it this way I do not mean to downplay the cruciality of conversion or of the responsibility of Christians to witness to Jesus Christ that they too might enter into his life and that of the gathered community.

The biblical Kingdom

The Gospels stress this priority but put things differently. Initially, John the Baptist spoke of the coming of the Kingdom in apocalyptic terms: One was coming whom God would enable suddenly to intervene in human affairs, separate the righteous from the wicked, and establish a Kingdom that would stand for ever. After John's arrest, however, Jesus spoke differently. The earlier theme: 'Repent, for the kingdom of heaven is at hand' (Matt 3:2) was now prefaced with a pointed reference to the immediate present: 'The time has come. The kingdom of God is near' (Mark 1:15). By these and many other words he specified that in his own person the Kingdom was 'near'. Indeed, Jesus boldly projected himself into the servant role of Yahweh, and began to carry out its predicted ministries (Luke 4:18–21 with Isa 35:1–10; 61:1–4). The Kingdom was no longer solely a future hope but a present reality. Whereas John's disciples had mourned and fasted, Jesus' disciples did not (Mark 2:18–19). His 'kingly rule' with its concepts of community and fellowship was essentially a power at work in the present, 'exercising its force'. It also concerned a community, a house, an area 'where the goods of salvation are available and received'.[23] It precipitated 'a violent and impetuous thronging to gather around Jesus and His disciples' (Hort on Matt 11:12). It 'came upon' people (Matt 12:28) and was a veritable presence 'among' them (Luke 17:20–21). Truly, in Jesus the old order of forward-looking hope yielded to a new order reflecting 'redemption accomplished' and guaranteeing the final triumph of God in history.

The Kingdom today

This is the startling distinctive of the messianic age. No longer are the people of God to be an encapsulated, worshipping community in the midst of the nations. They are to face outward, proclaim the presence of the Kingdom by word and deed, and issue the call to conversion. When they catch a vision of the kingdom of God, they begin to acquire Jesus' perspectives on the poor, the orphan, the widow, the refugee, the wretched of the earth, and to embrace his concern for justice, mercy, and truth — not a preoccupation with church affairs but a kingdom vision that is all-embracing. Snyder describes the contrast in the following fashion:

> Church people think about how to get people into the church; Kingdom people think about how to get the church into the world. Church people worry that the world might change the church; Kingdom people work to see the church change the world ... If the church has one great need, it is this: To be set free for the Kingdom of God, to be liberated from itself as it has become in order to be itself as God intends. The church must be freed to participate fully in the economy of God.[24]

Evangelicals here and there are increasingly coming to sense that the kingdom of God motif provides what Johannes Verkuyl has called 'the hub around which all of mission work revolves' and adds, 'We who practice mission must take the Kingdom of God as our constant point of orientation. It is imperative that we pay close heed to the whole range of burdens and evils plaguing mankind'.[25] If God's tomorrow means the end of exploitation, injustice, inequality, war, racism, nationalism, suffering, death, and the ignorance of God, Christians must be 'signs' today of God's conquest of all these 'burdens and evils' through the Cross and Resurrection of Jesus Christ. No longer can evangelicals confine themselves to the single priority of proclaiming the knowledge of God among the nations and settle for the status quo of everything else. Of course, Christians shall not establish the Kingdom, much less bring it to fullness. Any biblical theology of mission worth its salt will show that God alone will accomplish this. The consummation of human history and the manifestation of the Kingdom in power and glory will be the work of God alone. But this does not mean that Christians today dare indulge the luxury of indifference to the moral and social issues of today. Only those are 'blessed' who are the merciful, the peacemakers, the persecuted for righteousness' sake: 'Theirs is the kingdom of heaven' (Matt 5:7–12).

The relation of all this to conversion is obvious. Jim Wallis speaks for us all when he says:

I have steadily become more convinced that understanding
conversion is really the central issue for today's churches.
Conversion understood apart from or outside history must be
reappropriated and understood in direct relationship to that
history.[26]

The call to conversion is a call to discipleship. And it can have no other
centre than the kingdom of God. It involves participation in the life, worship, and service of a community committed to an active discipleship in the
world.[27]

When we issue the call to conversion we must make abundantly clear
what the Kingdom is all about. And the issue of issues is whether people
are willing to follow Jesus and be publicly identified with his Kingdom. As
Wallis states:

> Evangelism confronts each person with the decisive choice
> about Jesus and the Kingdom, and it challenges the oppres-
> sion of the old order with the freeing power of a new one. The
> gospel of the Kingdom sparks a fundamental change in every
> life and is an intrusion into any social order, be it first-century
> culture or our twentieth-century world.[28]

Conclusion

We could have confined our discussion to the significant evidences of God
at work in the world today; the 'critical mass' that was achieved by his
grace in China so that the spontaneous expansion of the Christian movement there is at a rate greater than anywhere else in the world; of the
growing positive ferment regarding conversion in the Orthodox churches;
of the growth rate of evangelical churches in Japan currently exceeding
the growth of comparable churches in the USA; of the growing spirit of
inquiry among significant Muslim groups in the Middle East and in
Indonesia; of the growing spirit of religious inquiry in metropolitan France
and the French-speaking peoples in Africa and Madagascar; of the radical
reconstruction of several influential American missionary societies working in Europe in response to recent evidences of spiritual awakening
within the older, established or 'state' churches; of the continuing growth
of Third World mission societies eager to penetrate hitherto unreached
peoples; of the positive aids to mission arising from increasingly pluralistic
religious situations in the West; of the remarkable increase in Jewish
response to the claims of Jesus Christ spearheaded by Jews who quite
openly confess their unwillingness to be regarded as non-Jews merely

because of their confession of him as their Messiah; of the worldwide phenomenon of a growing missionary consciousness among Christian Chinese, scattered as they are in significant numbers in more than 80 countries; of the continued increase of charismatic Christians in a host of separate movements in major segments of Latin America, South Asia, and the West; and of the growing lay movements within the Roman Catholic Church (*comunidades de base*) seeking to emphasise Bible study, conversion, and evangelistic outreach. God is indeed at work today on a thousand fronts that he might consummate his world mission tomorrow.

Of course, the Devil is at work too, and his growing challenge to the Christian church must not be minimised. We dare not dismiss any of his 'isms' as harmless, for this would be to underestimate the power of the Evil One. Neither should we regard any 'ism' as too mighty a giant in the land, for this would be to underestimate Christ's conquest of all powers. The Devil is indeed at work today.

But the crucial question is whether we are at work. We dare not just stand before our generation and 'explain' the gospel to its peoples. We are to preach it instead and issue the call to conversion. Jesus Christ is not merely to be proclaimed that he might be admired. He is to be responded to. Jesus Christ is Lord.

Notes

1 Arnold van Gennep, *The Rites of Passage* (University of Chicago Press: Chicago, 1960), p 96.
2 Richard Crossman, *The God that Failed* (Harper and Row: New York, 1950), Bantam Matrix edition p 19.
3 Emil Brunner, *The Great Invitation* (Westminster Press: Philadelphia, 1955), pp 105, 100.
4 Hugh T Kerr and John M Mulder, *Conversions: The Christian Experience* (Eerdmans: Grand Rapids, 1983).
5 For details on historical factors see ch 6, Harris; cultural factors see ch 5, Newbigin; mass evangelism chs 8 and 11, Brierley and Pointer.
6 Quoted by Leighton Ford, 'Conversion: God's Climax and Man's Crisis' (unpublished paper presented at the Ecumenical Evangelism Conference of the National Council of Churches: Green Lake, Wisconsin, 1967), p 7.
7 Kerr and Mulder, *op cit*.
8 Paul G Hiebert, 'Missions and the Renewal of the Church', in Wilbert R Shenk, ed, *Exploring Church Growth* (Eerdmans: Grand Rapids, 1983), p 157.
9 Aylward Shorter, *African Christian Theology: Adaptation or Incarnation?* (Maryknoll/Orbis Books, 1977), p 10.
10 'The Willowbank Report: Gospel and Culture', *Lausanne Occasional Papers*, no 2 (Lausanne Committee for World Evangelization: Charlotte, NC, 1978), p 21.
11 George Bradford Caird, *Principalities and Powers: A Study in Pauline Theology*

(Clarendon Press: Oxford, 1956), p x.

12 Hendrikus Berkhof, *Christ and the Powers*, trans by J H Yoder (Herald Press: Scottdale, 1962), p 22.

13 Heinrich Schlier, *Principalities and Powers in the New Testament* (Herder and Herder: New York, 1961), p 38.

14 Caird, *op cit*, p 53.

15 Berkhof, *op cit*, p 23.

16 Berkhof, *op cit*, p 26.

17 Alan R Tippett, *Verdict Theology in Missionary Theory* (Lincoln Christian College: Lincoln, IL, 1969), pp 89, 90.

18 Paul G Hiebert, 'The Flaw of the Excluded Middle', *Missiology: An International Review*, vol 10, no 1 (January 1982): p 35.

19 *ibid*, p 46.

20 Howard Snyder, *Liberating the Church* (Inter-Varsity Press: Downers Grove, IL, 1983).

21 Quoted by Ford, *op cit*.

22 Paul Loffler, 'Conversion in an Ecumenical Context', *The Ecumenical Review*, vol 19, no 3 (July 1967): p 257.

23 Aslen Svere, '"Reign" and "House" in the Kingdom of God in the Gospels', *New Testament Studies*, vol 8 (1961), p 223.

24 Snyder, *op cit*. p 11.

25 Johannes Verkuyl, *Contemporary Missiology* (Eerdmans: Grand Rapids, 1978), p 203.

26 Jim Wallis, *The Call to Conversion* (Lion: Tring, 1981), p xvi.

27 Jose Miguez Bonino, 'Conversion. New Creature and Commitment', *International Review of Mission*, vol 72 no 287 (July 1983): p 331.

28 Wallis, *op cit*, p 17.

4
the impact of conversion
CHRISTOPHER SUGDEN

Chris Sugden is Registrar of the Oxford Centre for Mission Studies, which enables Christian leaders from the Two-Thirds World to do research on mission in their own context, using the academic resources available in the West. He worked with the church in India for a number of years and published several books with his senior colleague, Vinay Samuel, as well as Radical Discipleship *(Marshalls), and* Christ's Exclusive Claims *and* Inter-Faith Dialogue *(Grove Booklets). He begins his contribution with a study of the psychological impact of conversion. He devotes the main section to an understanding of the Kingdom of God; here he draws on his cross-cultural experience. He concludes by outlining strategies that have enabled the gospel to be preached effectively to the poor.*

The impact of conversion on whom?

Almost half of all the 97,000 people who went forward at the Billy Graham meetings in 1984–85 were students. The Luis Palau Mission to London showed the same sort of figures — startling indeed![1] What was good about the Good News to those students? In what way was the Good News presented so that it brought that response from that particular group? To answer these questions we have to discover what problems and needs the Good News addressed.

Students seem to have much in common. They typify the ideal person in our culture. They are single, unattached, upwardly mobile, usually childless, with few if any family commitments. Students are what many people would like to be, and what marketing firms tell us we are or ought to be. One need many students have in common with many others in our society is that they are lonely. A young person on Radio 4's *Thought for the Day* described all his problems and then put the cause down to loneliness — lost in a crowd, lack of direction, no signposts. And again my local paper recently announced the formation of a new group called 'SALI' ('SALI' means Single and Loving It). It has about 4,000 members who were arranging a meeting in the Town Hall because they wanted to meet together. There seems to be a slight contradiction! Nevertheless, it says an awful lot about our society. One in four people in London lives alone by choice. At a consultation in the United States about urban ministry,[2] one church leader from New York said 75% of his congregation lived alone by choice.

The gospel has been largely formulated in our Western culture within the context of the *individual* life. Conversion stories are often in terms of individual struggles, individual histories, how some intellectual questions are resolved and how the gospel brings a degree of self-affirmation. The latter is important in our context with all the pressures on the individual. But Britain is a powerful nation able to export ideas by trade, by people — scientists, missionaries, and so on. We have universalised the individual faith and said that *that* is the context of faith for *everybody*.

This was dramatically brought home to me in a small Indian village. We spent 10 days with some Indian seminary students, working with a small group of villagers. At the end we had a small celebration in which there was a drama and singing, and then finally one of the students gave a short message, that Jesus was the answer to his loneliness, and could be the answer to theirs. The student had imposed on the villagers the needs which the gospel had answered for him. We do the same. These villagers, about 50 of them, lived in two streets. They were all intermarried and probably had never travelled more than 50 miles in their lives. Loneliness was not their problem.

My senior colleague, Vinay Samuel, was sharing what happened when he met with a group of Christian leaders in north-east India. He reports that during a discussion about the barriers to evangelism in north-east India, one of the church leaders got up and said:

> One of the barriers now for evangelism among us is that we are one of the most corrupt states in India. 80% of us are Christians and yet corruption is rife. It is well known that Mrs Gandhi won the elections in Nagaland about four or five years ago through bribes, and the bribes were received by Christians. One of the problems for evangelism in our context is that the state collector of taxes will receive bribes on Saturday and then go and preach on Sunday. What has happened among us

is that we have separated spiritual transformation from transformation in society. We have separated off the individual from the community. We believe that if we have got spiritual transformation all other transformation of relationships will automatically follow. And it just does not work.

It is not only a question of whether it works or not. The question is whether imposing the individual context of faith on everyone is actually biblical; whether defining evangelism and conversion in purely individual terms owes more to our culture than to Scripture. Our culture is deeply shaped by the Enlightenment. Bishop Newbigin has vividly pointed out that the Enlightenment has as its model of human life the individual who owes nothing to anybody.[3] He is independent; how embarrassed we are when we have to ask for help. The individual makes his own decisions; how bad we feel when we have no choice in matters, when we are just told to do things and there is no option. The individual has a whole range of options before him and can choose anything; our consumer economy is geared to giving us massive choices. Our culture is deeply influenced by that Enlightenment vision of the individual independent person, who accepts no authority over him or her. Conversion has been structured to fit into that.

We hear so many conversion testimonies and read books that tell about how people who were under pressure had to be successful, to show that they were independent and maintain the façade. They were under pressure on their marriage, their health, their relationships and their family. They had reached breaking point, when Jesus came in and helped them survive so that they could maintain and fulfil that goal of the successful individual. Conversion has not led them to question the model. Conversion is recommended because it can enable us to achieve the model our society holds before us.

Many other pressures are there. According to Robert Banks time, not money, is the god of our society.[4] Alvin Toffler in *The Third Wave*[5] says that the coming of the Industrial Revolution, with mass production, puts the manufacturing process into the relentless time schedule of machinery. Our life is controlled by time.

Understanding the Kingdom

The impact of conversion is often wrongly limited by culture, but it must always be rightly relevant to culture. How can we distinguish between the bone and marrow of those two things? Dr George Carey writes about the turning around involved in conversion.[6] Turning around to what? If we look at the preaching of John the Baptist and Jesus in Matthew (3:1–12 and 4:12–17), turning around was in relationship to the kingdom of God. A new reality had invaded the world. A new rule had been declared, or rather, an old rule had been affirmed, the kingdom of God. God rules. We turn around and orientate our lives and values not to the values of society, not to the values affirmed by the Pharisees which were that we should be wise, first, great and rich; instead, we should orientate our lives to the values of the Kingdom. These were that God revealed things to fools and to babes; the first shall be last, the least shall be the greatest, and blessed are the poor. Orientate our lives to the Kingdom. Turn around to that.

The gospel does not stand alone. It is the Good News of the Kingdom. When the preaching of John and of Jesus is summarised by Matthew, and when the gospel is defined by Luke, it is the gospel of the Kingdom. Though Paul mentions the gospel without the qualifying phrase of the Kingdom, we must always remember that the content of the gospel defined by Paul is the content given and defined by Jesus: the Good News of the Kingdom. The Kingdom has arrived. Repentance therefore is in relationship to the Kingdom.

So if the gospel is the Good News of the Kingdom, the Kingdom is the context for conversion, the context within which people must repent and into which people must enter. We cannot enter the kingdom of God unless we are born again; in fact we cannot even see it (see John 3:3). So the Kingdom is the context where relationships are transformed. Jesus brings new relationships; new relationships with God (they call him *Abba*, Father), new relationships with other people especially people who belong to alien groups (Jews and Gentiles are brothers and sisters in Christ); new relationships with the physical creation, healing and resurrection. It is in the light of that context that we must understand the language of conversion.

In John 3 the language of being born again is in the context of an invitation to enter the Kingdom. No one can enter the kingdom of God unless he is born of water and the Spirit (3:5). To be born again is not an end in itself: it is only a sign that a person recognises that he or she has entered the kingdom of God. The great temptation is to make being born again itself the whole context rather than just the doorway. We do not talk about the whole room which is the Kingdom and in which all relationships are being transformed.

Repentance is then related to the Kingdom. It is about the need to turn about because the Kingdom has come. Mark introduced Jesus' preaching with a summary, 'The time has come. The kingdom of God is near. Repent and believe the good news!' (Mark 1:14). The Jews were called to repent by Jesus because they had no belief that God would actually act in the present. They believed that he would come one day in the future, but he was not active now.

The repentance to which John the Baptist called people was to turn from the misuse of resources and the abuse of power by petty officials. The Pharisees were called to repent because they privatised morality and separated the Law from compassion and from justice. They said God was not at work to deliver the people of Israel from Roman rule because many Jews were impure and racially mixed. They blamed private personal sins for the social situation of the nation. They identified certain people as sinners — a technical term of abuse. The Pharisees said that because there were still sinners who broke the Law, God had not sent his Messiah and had not delivered Israel from the Roman rule. In other words, the Pharisees were doing the time-honoured job of blaming the victim, and they did so because they did not expect God to be at work in the midst of their community. They only expected that at that time God was at work in individual lives; hence all the blame had to attach to individuals.

Our gospel can be misheard so badly. If we tell people who have been told all their lives that they are sinners that the Good News to them is that they are sinners through their own fault, we are telling them nothing new. To tell outcast people in India that they are sinners is to tell them nothing different from what the Brahmins have been telling them all their lives, that it is their fault that they are poor. So the starting-point of the Good News for those people is that God loves them. Jesus says, 'I've come to call sinners.' The Pharisees would have expected him to say, 'I've come to condemn sinners.' That is how our gospel can be misheard. The Kingdom is misunderstood as an essentially personal matter which grows as more and more individuals respond to Jesus. That is actually a distortion of the biblical presentation. It privatises the Kingdom to a merely personal impact. The Kingdom is about a new reality come to transform *all* relationships and is the fulfilment of God's purpose in creation.

Transformation

The term increasingly used to describe this process is the term 'transformation'. A consultation at Wheaton defined transformation thus:

> According to the biblical view of human life, then, transformation is the change from a condition of human existence contrary to God's purposes to one in which people are able to enjoy fulness of life in harmony with God (John 10:10; Col 3:8–15; Eph 4:13). This transformation can only take place through the obedience of individuals and communities to the Gospel of Jesus Christ, whose power changes the lives of men and women by releasing them from the guilt, power and consequences of sin, enabling them to respond with love toward God and towards others (Rom 5:5) and making them 'new creatures in Christ' (II Cor 5:17).[7]

That description tries to define how the Church is to respond to human needs. Does it just give aid? Does it try to bring development which actually harnesses poor nations to Western models of economic growth? Or does the Church actually have something unique to say about human relationships? This concept of transformation was thus developed to include different aspects of the way God brings change.

First, change must affirm God's activity without undermining the role of people. Some affirm that only God brings change, and that is right. This is taken to extreme by saying he will only bring change at the end of history. This is an apocalyptic, intertestamental view. It is not the view of the Kingdom. Others insist that change can only come as people demand change themselves. God does call us to be co-workers with him. But if we affirm only that people must bring change then we condemn people to pulling themselves up by their own bootstraps.

Second, transformation speaks of the need for value change in the hearts of people and in the hearts of systems. The fundamental change in values is central to any lasting change. The Christian basis for this is given in Colossians 3. Paul asserts there that because of the Resurrection, the values of Jesus Christ — compassion, kindness, humility, gentleness and patience — are the values which are in heaven where Christ sits on his throne. Those values must be in the hearts of people but they must also be in the heart of systems. Many systems and structures are harsh and unjust. In India the caste system makes quick work of dehumanising people. Individuals in India are captive to a system which requires people to treat others as less than human. Change in that situation requires not only change in the hearts of individuals, but change in the heart of the system. This means that as we work to affirm people's values which the Bible affirms and to challenge the values the Bible criticises, we are pointing to the lordship of Christ. For Christ is the guarantee of those values, and people need his power to live by them. Beginning with change in people's values is a witness to the nature of, and need for, submitting to Christ as Lord.

Good News for the poor

We can be more specific. This Kingdom is Good News for the poor. In Luke 4:18 Jesus 'found the place' in Isaiah to define his ministry. 'He has anointed me to preach good news to the poor.' When Jesus was replying to the messengers of John the Baptist (Luke 7:22), he gave the authentication of his ministry. 'Go back and report to John what you have seen and heard.' He referred again to Isaiah's prophecy of the Messiah. 'The blind receive sight, the lame walk, those who have leprosy are cured, the deaf hear, the dead are raised, and the good news is preached to the poor.' The

authentication for Jesus' messiahship was that the Good News was proclaimed to the poor. It was not — initially — Good News for Herod or the
Pharisees. Herod wanted to get rid of Jesus. The Pharisees kept on sending spies to follow Jesus around and trick him. But Luke tells us it was the
crowd (ochlos)[8] who heard him gladly, who went out to him, who followed
him round the lake, who turned up to be fed, who brought their sick to
him. They were the mob, the outcasts, the marginalised, the poor — and
it is Good News for them. The group studying *Reaching the Urban Poor* at
the Pattaya Consultation in 1980 made a very thorough biblical investiga-
tion of terms referring to the poor in Scripture. They came to the conclu-
sion that the poor in Scripture refers to

> the manual worker who struggles to survive on a day to day
> basis, the destitute cowering as a beggar, the one reduced to
> meekness, the one brought low ... those weak and tired from
> carrying heavy burdens, the leper and very often the common
> people ... the majority of references indicate that the poor are
> the mercilessly oppressed, the powerless, the destitute, the
> downtrodden.[9]

The relationship between the poor and the poor in spirit in Luke and in
Matthew's versions of the Beatitudes was that those who were poor had
no one to turn to for help but God. It did not mean they were saved. It
meant that — since they could not depend on the King for help (because
the King was often leading the attack against them rather like Ahab steal-
ing Naboth's vineyard), or on the process of law (because that had been
subverted, and Isaiah talks of those who practised mischief by statute) —
they were open to the real King. Poor in spirit does not mean spiritually
bankrupt, atheist, or impoverished in spiritual existence. It means open to
God, primarily, because of being oppressed. It means an attitude to God
that characterises those who are open to His help because they cannot
depend on help from anybody else. Jesus made the poor the focus of his
ministry. He goes to Galilee, the place of the low-class Jew, defined as
Galilee of the Gentiles. He spent his time among the socially outcast, the
women, the tax collectors, the sick who had been unable to work and
would also have been economically poor and socially outcast, believed to
be punished by God; among the contaminated, the lepers, and the ochlos
— the crowd.

Jesus' focus continued the focus of God's work in the Old Testament to
redeem creation. Israel was the place where the nations could see the
character, the activity and the purpose of God. What God did for Israel,
what God rewarded, what God punished in Israel was to be the definition
of what he was doing for everyone. God's will for Israel reveals God's will
for mankind. God loves the world, but defines the nature and meaning of

that love through his focus on Israel. The children of Israel were the migrant, dispossessed landless labourers in Pharaoh's Egypt. They were subject to cruel task masters. They had loathsome working conditions, and they were subject to a vicious birth control policy. They suffered from Pharaoh's sin which was to exercise the very dominion over people which God had given men and women over creation but not over each other.

In restoring his creation God began by rescuing those poor people from the sin of Pharaoh. He gave them land — a place. He gave them laws to prevent such oppression within their own community. Their creed was not to make philosophical statements about God, or psychological statements about their own contentment. It was to make statements about what God had done in history in delivering them from Pharaoh's oppression. The context of faith for Israel was God's work in history. 'My father was a wandering Aramean; we went down into Egypt; Pharaoh oppressed us; God redeemed us and gave us this land. Therefore I now bring this offering' — summarises Deuteronomy 26:1–11. This was the focus of God's work which defined the meaning of his restoration for all people. Deuteronomy 7:7 emphasises the point. 'The Lord did not set his affection on you and choose you because you were more numerous than other peoples, for you were the fewest of all peoples.'

Paul echoes this thought in I Corinthians 1:26, 28:

> Not many of you were wise by human standards; not many were influential; not many were of noble birth ... God chose the lowly things of the world and the despised things — and the things that are not — to nullify the things that are.

The poor are the focus of the meaning of the Good News. What the Good News of the Kingdom means to the poor defines what it is to mean for everyone. We see this in the parable of the Pharisee and the tax collector.

To understand what justification by faith means to the outcast, marginalised, despised tax collector is to define also what it means to that pillar of society who would be on all our church boards: the Pharisee (Luke 18:9–14). And Paul does the same. Paul's mission strategy to reach the Jews was to make them jealous that the fulfilment of God's promise to his people in the Old Testament was now to be fulfilled in the Gentiles (Rom 11:13–15). Thus the New Testament's acid test of the life of a community is what that community does to the poor.

Jesus asked the Pharisees and the Sadducees about their relationships with the poor. He charged them if their interpretation of the law of the Sabbath oppressed people who wanted healing, or if their understanding of the Scriptures denigrated women as second-class citizens. Jesus' teaching on social ethics places poor and community together. Our individual context of faith has unfortunately limited faith to the spiritual dimension and to individual lives. We have to go back to the Scriptures again and learn from those who are poor their perspective on the gospel. We need it for our spiritual health, and for our own understanding of what the gospel is about.

Stewardship

Men and women are called to be in the image of God. Image means being the tenant of the invisible God, having dominion on his behalf, over creation (Gen 1:27–28). Our calling is also to be fashioned in the image of Christ, in the true image of God (Rom 8:29), who is the second Adam and the true steward/servant. That therefore means that the context of our discipleship is to be true stewards. Our Christian teaching on discipleship should include how to use resources properly, how to manage a family budget, how to enable people to set up small businesses, how to provide resources for Christian mission from businesses. This is happening in the Two-Thirds World. And yet in Britain we inherit a social situation in which trade is disparaged. In Britain we talk about reaching people in trade and business for Christ, but we talk little about Christian business practice.

The impact on our culture

What then is the impact of the Good News of the Kingdom in our culture? Jesus' way of doing this was to find a group, and to find a starting-point with that group. With the Pharisees it was their interpretation of the Law; with the Sadducees it was their understanding of power; with the poor it was whether they had the faith that Jesus could change things; with the rich it was whether they could respond to responsibility to the poor. In the Indian context, the issue for foraging rubbish pickers in Delhi was their identity. They were called 'nobodies'. After a group of Christians had worked with them for a year they had moved to realise that God called them to be Sons, in Christ. They no longer called themselves 'nobodies'.

What is our starting-point going to be in the many cultures of Britain? We have noted how for the middle classes individual fulfilment is the highest expression of life; time is important; people are devalued; status is very significant. Our culture makes us expect certain things to change with conversion. We expect it to enable us to achieve the goals and success that we cannot achieve alone, to bring individual self-affirmation. We do not expect it to alter those goals! We have a prosperity doctrine, and a blessing theology, which measures our standing with God according to the 'blessings' we receive. And this becomes Good News for us when it affirms society's values! We have found a starting-point for the gospel in our culture but not allowed that to be challenged by the gospel. Instead it has been its channel of the gospel.

Marketing strategies fit perfectly into the goal of our culture that conversion is meant to help us achieve. But marketing segments society because it defines us. For example, British Leyland produced a brochure which claimed that Minis are bought by single professional young ladies under 30; Metros by bank clerks starting a family. Maestros are bought by the middle-class professional, with three children. And so on up the ladder. Marketing categorises us. If we engage in the process of segmenting the market we are contributing to making people less than whole people. We will have young people's groups, old people's groups, single homeless groups and one-parent family groups. We will busily make ghettoes within our churches and in our society. Marketing simplifies things because it has to convey a message simply in as few words as possible. And therefore we are tempted to find an irreducible minimum for the gospel. But in marketing, when image is all, ethical issues are avoided. We must be aware of what our culture does. We therefore need new models for conversion.

Changing the model for conversion

We tend to operate in our society with an intellectual model for conversion. We try to make supernatural beliefs acceptable to rational minds. The books on apologetics are all about the intellectual reasons for faith. Is that the scriptural model of conversion? Or should we have a much more personal model of conversion — such as marriage? The Scripture uses the model of marriage in the Old Testament in Hosea and in the New Testament in Ephesians. We all have different starting-points for marriage: all the stories of how couples met are different. But we do not use them as reasons for saying, 'Well, you're not properly married because you didn't meet your husband in the right situation.' With a personal model, therefore, we can cope much better.

It's a social model, too, because we are introduced to a family. I was at the wedding of a black Christian in Los Angeles in 1984. In a beautiful ceremony the parents of the bride and groom were asked, 'Will you take this man to be your son?' 'Will you take this woman to be your daughter?' It was a marriage of families. Again, perhaps the model we should be working towards is based on social relationships rather than on the intellect.

Strategy for impact

Pilgrimage 2000 was a programme initiated by all the churches in India about four years ago to reach all the groups of people in India by the year 2000. They are developing a framework of strategy, as follows.

First, they identify a community or a group. The 1980 Consultation on World Evangelisation at Pattaya noted that people could be defined, understood or appreciated as members of a group that had something in common. In terms of their religious commitment, they were either Muslims, Hindus, traditional animists or nominal Roman Catholics; but in addition to the religious component, there was the social component, the economic component, and the race component. A poor Hindu would probably have more in common with a poor Muslim than either of them in common with a rich member of the same group of people. You might find a group of people who have things in common because they live in the same area, do the same type of work, live in the same place, or have the same interests.

Second, they identify the frontier of the gospel with that group. What is it about the life of the group which when compared with the life of the Kingdom is challenged by the gospel? The unemployed are a group of people who are not able to exercise their full human stewardship because they are out of work. Things in common have made them a group of people, whether they realise it or not.

The following case illustrates the method of Pilgrimage 2000. A group of Christian students was doing research among quarry workers living north of Bangalore. Over a couple of weeks, the students drew a profile of the people informally. As they became involved, they discovered a number of needs in that community — the men drank a lot and justified their behaviour thus: 'Well, if you do our work of carrying all this stone around, day in and day out, in the evenings you would drink, just to relax, forget, and have some sort of respite from this terribly hard work.' There is also illness around. And the children worked in the quarry and were pocked with sores from flying stone chips. There was no education for these children. The women worked, but they were also prostitutes to supplement the family income because the men drank the money they earned. It was not enough, though, to deal with the need, because beneath the needs were other issues. Drunkenness could not be tackled by the students' saying 'Don't drink' because the working conditions were the issue.

The students then looked at the children's health and asked why the parents didn't send their children to the nearby hospital. Sadly, the parents protested that nobody ever came back from the hospital alive. Convinced that hospitals could not help anyone, they had always consulted the spirits to find out where the 'evil spirit' was coming from. They then sacrificed a goat to appease it.

In this lay their insecurity. They felt that they were being attacked all round by unseen forces over which they had no control. They added that they were migrant workers from the next state. They did not belong to the area, nor did they speak the language. Having arrived 25 years ago, but still belonging to their villages 200 miles away, they returned there for all the major family celebrations. They did not own any land; they were just temporary residents at the quarry. They explained that if the quarry owner decided to sack them, he could. So there was tremendous insecurity among these migrant labourers.

The students had to look further still, for structures are built into any society. They are for the benefit of the people — but which people? The quarry contractor benefited from that particular structure of employment. The quarry workers were also trapped by their religious structure. Through a process of discussion, the students asked them what events would actually communicate God's love. They tried to discover the visions and hopes the quarry workers had for their community and worked with them to realise them, given that those visions were validated by the gospel. The students began to find out what events would make a difference to the life of the quarry workers. The group suggested that things would change if they could win the contract to work the quarry themselves. Then they would be employing themselves and would enjoy much greater security.

The gospel is about event and explanation. All the sermons in Acts arise out of events. The disciples started speaking in all Mediterranean languages in the middle of Jerusalem, then Peter preached a sermon. Peter and John healed the man at the gate Beautiful, which gave rise to two sermons. The sermons in Acts by and large arose out of events and happenings. In Mark, Jesus performed many miracles. People ask 'What is this new teaching?' So the presentation of the Good News of the Kingdom is through event and explanation. The problem is that in Western society under the challenge of the Enlightenment the Church has devoted tremendous amounts of energy to refining its explanations and then propagating its explanations. We tend not to give so much importance to the fact that these explanations must be prompted by and explain events of God's action in our midst.

The Christian team affirmed the quarry workers' desire for security in the light of the Bible. Had not God provided Israel with a land, a place to belong, and access to resources? So they began to work with the quarry workers towards their goal. They also began to pray with them for it. The quarry workers were not Christians but the Christian team worked from a number of biblical themes. First, the quarry workers were poor, and poor in spirit — as we have seen this means 'open to help from God.' Second, in Acts 14 we read how Paul affirmed that when the people of Lystra had prayed to Zeus, their prayers for crops and food had indeed been answered by the living God (Acts 14:14–18), but not by the one they thought had answered them. So Paul moved them on from where they were.

Prayer was part of these quarry workers' lives. They spent their time praying that God would not let them die. The Christian team suggested that they pray and work together for God to help them get the contract for the quarry. They prayed and made a bid. The result was that the contractor doubled their wages. Many would say that the quarry workers should have refused this offer and not allowed themselves to be bought off so easily. But the quarry workers accepted the offer. And they said: 'This is the first change for good that has ever happened in our lives. You Christians have taught us that this is the work of your God. So your God will be our God.' The impact on these people was immense. They had only known of a god who was continually punishing them for their sins with poverty, illness and suffering. Now something had happened which the Christians explained as the work of the God of Jesus, a God who wanted justice for poor people.

This represented the starting-point for these people to enter the life of the Kingdom. Of course there remained a whole wealth of Christian teaching and life to be explored. But the crucial point was to find the frontier or the starting-point.

We have seen that the gospel is about event and explanation. Biblically another event that requires explanation is the very existence of the Church as a cross-cultural mixed community of Jews and Gentiles. Margaret Mead forcused on this at the Nairobi Assembly of the World Council of Churches in 1975. She told all the delegates gathered from round the world that they were a sociological impossibility, because they had nothing in common as a group except their extraordinary belief that Jesus Christ was the Saviour of the world and had risen from the dead.

The events of Christ's life will not be crystal clear to all. The death and resurrection of Jesus did not convince Pilate or the Jews that he was the Messiah. God's acts can always be explained in different ways. But in the face of the Enlightenment's attempts to explain away God's actions in history, the Western church has tended to retreat, and not even attempt to affirm it. It has made God's action invulnerable to secular inspection and located it in the individual heart and experience. We have generally abandoned events in history as far as God's action is concerned. So our evangelism has often ended up as an explanation of psychological changes. We refine the explanations and use the technological tools of radio, mass media, etc, to broadcast these psychological changes as widely as possible. Again, though, we have tended to abandon the event in the life of the community which is relevant to the community's life and in which God's action is demonstrated.

This process of evangelism strategy has been written up as a 10-week course for use by groups.[10] Many groups who have gone through the course have said to me, 'We cannot break off this process of getting to know the community and identifying a frontier for the gospel with the end of the course. We are going to continue our involvement with them.'

To summarise, then, the process is first to make a community profile of an identifiable group. Second, when possible to identify with the group a frontier for the gospel, an event relevant to the frontier, and then to pray and work with the people in the group for an event.

Measuring that impact

The Scriptures give us the tools to measure the impact of the gospel and the impact of conversion. First, there is people's identity. In Christ we are given a new identity as sons and daughters of the living God. Being the owner of a brand new XJ6 is a false identity. Being defined as single, homeless and on welfare is an imposed identity; being defined as unemployed is to say that your identity is only found if you work. That is the scourge of Marxism which defined man as a worker, but it is not a biblical identity. The middle class is busy rushing to earn its identity. All the adverts on television are geared to a middle-class identity. The gospel of grace is that we are given a new identity as sons and daughters of God. This is a great liberation, whether we are denied an identity or have to strive to earn or preserve one.

Second, the gospel is about giving access to power — the power of God. Somebody who has worked all his life among tribal peoples and researched their response to Christianity has said their response was about the access to power. Is the power of God greater than the power of evil, and is the power of God available to them? Empowerment is also in terms of access to resources, in terms of decision making.

Third, are people enabled to be truly human by exercising the stewardship God has given them? While the welfare state is a very good thing, a problem with its operation is that it has created welfare dependency and does not go far enough in empowering people to create their own life. The welfare state at present encourages people more to be receivers and consumers than to be stewards. How can our church programmes move beyond trying to bolster up the welfare state to encourage people in stewardship?

A fourth mark of the impact of conversion is servanthood. In Matthew the parable of the talents is followed by the teaching of the Great Assize (Matt 25:14–46). In brief, its challenge is this: those who are made stewards of resources are to risk them in service of the master, and the way we serve the master Jesus is by serving him in his brothers: the poor, sick and imprisoned. Thus the challenge to the upwardly mobile is to use resources to enable those at the bottom of the pile to come up as well.

A fifth mark of the impact of conversion is commitment to the family. The social conduit for God-given change in society in the Scriptures is the family. The extended family is the basis for society and the focus of power in Israelite society in the Mosaic legislation.[11] In the New Testament it is interesting to note that Jesus instructed many people whom he had healed to 'go home'. Maybe that should feature more in discipleship teaching to new Christians. In the New Testament the Church is defined as the family of families. Paradoxically, we have churches where the pulpit says God is in favour of the family, but where the church programme splits up the family.

Families cannot be affirmed without resources. In the Scriptures the family is related to land and place. The Jubilee every 50 years meant going back to the family's place. A Baptist minister, Ray Bakke, said that he feels the inadequacy of an independent ecclesiology is that it neglects place and commitment to place as part of Christian involvement.[12] It can set up a house church of a local congregation anywhere and yet is not committed to place; and that has led to the flight of the churches from the inner city. Bakke also noted that historically the churches that have remained in the inner city after 25 years have been the churches experiencing renewal — because they had a theology of place. That was God's place for them. The numbers did not matter; that was where they had to be faithful.

Sixth, the Good News for the whole world is to be focused on what it means to the poor. The agenda of the poor, then, is to be the agenda of all our churches. An international seminar on evangelism and the poor produced a report in 1981 on what such an agenda of the poor would look like. These were their suggestions:

1. The poor should shape the content of the gospel that the middle-class holds.

2. Many middle-class people are actually in solidarity with the poor and are working with all their skills and abilities to bring about struggle and salvation.

3. The Church as a whole should change in the direction of the church of the poor, where the poor feel at home in terms of worship, the understanding of the Scriptures, solidarity and oneness; where they feel that they also own the church and have a share in responsibility in the church.

4. If we can find a way in which the middle-class can begin to share the concerns of the poor, then we have something genuine. The middle-class church can provide the resources that we need in the struggle with the poor. This can transform the middle-class church. It will involve suffering. Once the Church commits itself to the poor, then it shares their burdens. The image of the church of

the middle-class which the poor hold is that it does not want to get into trouble. Let the Church open the door, and become exposed and vulnerable because the agenda of the poor is on its table.

5. In areas where there is no absolute poverty, the poor do not care for the money of middle-class Christians. What they care for is power. They want middle-class Christians to be useful. In India certain middle-class groups are deeply involved in organising people against oppression. Suppose they say to us: 'You are middle-class people. You are far more useful to us where you are. You are more useful as a church which speaks on our behalf, by remaining where you are. You can make your resources available to us and use your power at times on our behalf.' Would we not be responding to their agenda if we did as they asked us?

6. In India most church members are poor. Yet the established churches have geared their resources for the elite. The identity, the needs and aspirations of the church members are not being taken care of. They are being prostituted, exploited and made use of by the leadership not to care for their own people but to do something to maintain their institutions. So though the Indian church is a church of poor people, it cannot be called the church of the poor. It does not reflect the aspirations of the poor. Therefore to say that the Church in India is the church of the poor because sociologically it is made up of poor people is not helpful in missiological terms. It cannot preserve middle-class institutions and also claim to be the church of the poor.

This does not mean that all middle-class churches must become poor and be among the poor, nor that every member of the Church becomes poor. But the Church must adopt the agenda, concerns and destiny of the poor.[13]

Seventh and finally, in the context both of ministry among the poor and among the middle class, there is the whole issue of the relationship with the supernatural. Paul Hiebert at Fuller Theological Seminary has done major work on the phenomenon of folk religion among poor people.[14] While poor people may *nominally* be adherents of major world religions, their actual religious practice as regards the practical concerns of everyday life is in the field of folk religion, spirit worship, ancestor worship, astrology, etc. Dr Hiebert is drawing on his researches on this in India to address the whole area of spiritualism and occultism in the United States. Too often, these are the real attempts of poor people to have some access to power. The crucial issue is whether the Christian gospel can address these issues of the power of the supernatural, and in so doing whether it releases that power for the benefit of those for whom Jesus exercised power, the powerless. Can this concern for the release of supernatural power have real impact for the powerless in Handsworth and other inner-city areas who have had to resort to violent uses of power?

Conclusion

What is good about the Good News? We must hear the challenge of the Scripture to us about what is good about the Good News. The Kingdom sets the context. We must hear the challenge that comes to us from the experiences of poor Christians, who are the bearers of the meaning of the good news to us. For this challenge will be crucial to our grasp of the gospel that we share and to the gospel's grasp of us.

Notes

1 See Philip Back, *Mission England: What Really Happened?* (MARC Europe: London, 1986), pp 15, 27; and Peter Brierley, *Mission to London, Phase II: Who Went Forward?* (MARC Europe: London, 1986), pp 20–23.

2 Consultation on Urban Ministry: Overseas Ministries Study Centre, Ventnor, New Jersey, April 1985.

3 Lesslie Newbigin, *The Other Side of 1984* (British Council of Churches: London, 1984).

4 Robert Banks, *The Tyranny of Time* (Paternoster Press: Exeter, 1985).

5 Alvin Toffler, *The Third Wave* (Pan Books: London, 1980).

6 See Chapter 2 'A Biblical Perspective', pp 9–21.

7 'Social Transformation: The Church in Response to Human Need', *Transformation*, vol 1, no 4 (1984): pp 23–27.

8 The word *ochlos* means 'a mob'. See the New Testament study of the term by Ahn Byung Mhu in 'Jesus and the Minjung in the Gospel of Mark', Vinay Samuel and Christopher Sugden, eds, *Evangelism and the Poor* (Paternoster Press: Exeter, 1984), pp 67ff.

9 See *Christian Witness to the Urban Poor* (Lausanne Committee for World Evangelization, 1983). Published also in Samuel and Sugden, *op cit*, pp 46–47.

10 *The Gospel to the Whole Person* (TAFTEE, PO Box 520, Cooke Town, Bangalore 560005, India).

11 See C J W Wright, 'The Ethical Relevance of Israel as a State', *Transformation*, vol 1, no 4, p 11.

12 Ray Bakke at a public meeting at the London Institute for Contemporary

Christianity, September 1985.

13 Samuel and Sugden *op cit*, pp 147–48.

14 Paul Hiebert, 'Folk Religion in Andra Pradesh' in Samuel and Sugden, *op cit*.

5
a british and european perspective

LESSLIE NEWBIGIN

Bishop Lesslie Newbigin was a missionary in India for about 38 years, 6 years of which he was with the International Missionary Council and the World Council of Churches. He is now pastoring a multi-racial church in Birmingham. He too concentrates on the Kingdom of God, but from a rather different perspective than that of the previous chapter. He concentrates on the renewing of the mind and reflects on what is involved for contemporary British people when they take Romans 12:2 seriously. He looks at the historical lessons to be learnt from the Enlightenment and the more recent lessons to be learnt from the USA. He sees much of our Christianity as syncretistic in that it accepts marginalisation in a private world of 'values', while leaving unchallenged a public world of 'facts', supposed to be independent of the character and purpose of God. He believes that conversion must relate to our whole lifestyle, and that it is only then that we shall be able to enter the Kingdom.

The good news of the kingdom of God

Any systematic thought about conversion must begin, I think, with the call to conversion which was — according to Mark — the beginning of the public ministry of our Lord. 'Jesus went into Galilee, proclaiming the good news of God. "The time has come," he said. "The kingdom of God is near. Repent and believe the good news"' (Mark 1:14–15). And the call to repent and believe is immediately followed (in the next verse) by the call 'Follow me.'

The Greek word translated 'repent' is *metanoeite* which means literally 'change of mind, think again'. As George Carey has pointed out in his detailed word study above (pp 9–21), this involves a turning (or rather returning) to God, so here it is a turning to face the new fact which is announced as good news — namely, that the kingdom of God is at hand. This is news, the announcement of a new fact. It is not the launching of a programme. It is not the promulgation of a new religion. It is strictly a news release — the announcement of a new fact. Of course the idea that God reigns was not a new idea for the people of Israel. It was, and is, the central message of the Old Testament, announced in the Prophets, celebrated in the Psalms. What, then, is new? It is the fact that the kingship of God is no longer simply an idea, no longer a theological concept, no longer something far away in another world or in the remote future. The new fact is that this kingship, this sovereign rule of God is now a present reality with which you have to come to terms. It is present in Jesus. This is the Good News, the gospel.

When I served as a missionary in India, I used to get rather tired of the question that visitors used infallibly to put at some point or other: 'Are you optimistic or pessimistic about the prospects of Christianity in India?' This was such a standard question that I had eventually to develop a standard reply: 'I believe that Jesus rose from the dead, so the question does not arise.' You can be optimistic or pessimistic about a *programme*; but about a *fact* you are not optimistic or pessimistic: you are either believing or unbelieving. And this gospel, this good news, is — I repeat — not the launching of a programme but the announcement of a fact.

I ask you: is it not true that even believers are often conned by the media into thinking that Christianity is a programme, a 'good cause' which needs our support, which is going to collapse if we don't hurry up and do something to revive it? I find even evangelical Christians writing about 'whether Christianity has a future'. What nonsense!

U-turn

Now it is in relation to the announcement of this new fact that the call to repent, to be turned round, to be converted follows. Jesus says: 'Turn round and believe.' If you are facing the wrong way, of course you cannot recognise the new reality. There has to be a total U-turn of the mind, a radical turning round, a conversion. Only then is it possible to believe the new reality which is announced — that God's reign is now present in this man Jesus.

I remember a visit to an Indian village congregation which was remote from any road, which had to be reached on foot by crossing a river. You could enter the village either from the north or from the south, according

to which of the two possible crossing places you chose. The congregation
had decided that I would come from the south. They had prepared the sort
of reception that only an Indian village congregation can: there were gar-
lands, trays of fruit, musical instruments of all kinds, a choir, fireworks
and sword-dancers, all waiting to welcome the bishop. Unfortunately I
happened to come into the village at the other end, and found a few goats
and hens. Of course there was a crisis. I had to retreat hastily to give time
to the entire village to reorient itself, do a complete U-turn, face the other
way. Then I reappeared and was duly received. That is a good illustration
of what the call to conversion means in this first announcement of the
Good News. There *is* a new fact. But as long as you are facing in the wrong
direction, as long as you are expecting the reign of God to be something
other than what it really is, you will never be able to believe. Without that
radical conversion it is inconceivable that you should be able to recognise
the presence of the reign of God in this humble man, that you should be
able to see in the cross on Calvary, not defeat and shame but the power
and the wisdom and the glory of God. Without this radical turning round
of the whole mind it is simply inconceivable. That is why Paul says that the
word of the Cross is scandal to the godly and nonsense to the clever; that
is why those terrible chapters which form the centre of John's Gospel
show us that even the most devout and godly teachers of Israel could in the
end see nothing in Jesus but a blasphemer; that is why, among all the Old
Testament texts quoted in the New, the one most often quoted is the terrible word of Isaiah 6 which tells us that the word of God will be totally
incomprehensible to those for whom it is sent. And that is why Paul urges
his Roman readers to be 'transformed by the renewing of your mind'
(Rom. 12:2). That radical conversion of the mind is the precondition for
belief (a conversion which only God the Holy Spirit can accomplish) will
enable us to know in the weakness and foolishness of the Cross, the power
and the wisdom of God — the presence, in other words — of the Kingdom, the rule of God. Conversion involves the conversion of the will and
of the emotions, but only so as it also involves the conversion of the mind,
that radical U-turn which alone can enable us to see things as they truly
are.

An example from India

Why do I lay such stress on this in a chapter on 'Entering the Kingdom: a
British and European Perspective'? Let me try to explain. I have spent
most of my life as a missionary in India. As a foreigner living in India and
seeking to understand its religion and culture, I became aware of the
enormous power of beliefs which, for the most part, are hardly discussed
or thought about. They are the preconditions of thought, the unques-

tioned axioms. They are just 'how things are'. I refer, especially, to the doctrines of *Karma* and rebirth, and the doctrine of *Maya*. These together form a coherent whole within which you can understand human life in a rational way. Human life is part of the natural cycle of birth, growth, decay, death and new birth. All nature as we know it moves in this cyclical pattern. Consequently no contingent event in history can possibly embody eternal truth. No issue is ever finally settled; it will always come up again in another form. There are no final decisions. All that has been will be again. This very rational and coherent way of understanding human life has endured for millennia and none of the great movements of renewal and revolt, from the Buddha onwards, has called it in question. It is just 'how things are'.

Syncretism

Within this world-view there can be a very honourable place for Jesus. He is one of the great *jeevanmuktas*, those in whom ultimate reality has been realised. In the hall of the Ramakrishna Mission where I used to go every week to study with Hindu friends, there was a picture of Jesus along with those of other great holy men. On the great Christian festivals special honours would be paid to him before this picture. A Western missionary looking at this will cry 'syncretism', and of course he will be right. Even if the pictures of Jesus were to be multiplied a thousandfold and worship offered to them every week, that would not be the conversion of India. The basic world-view remains unchallenged. There has been no conversion.

Why do I talk about this? Because I want to affirm that British Christianity is profoundly syncretistic, and that we shall not be facing the question of conversion in the British context seriously if we do not face this fact. Let me try to explain what I mean.

World of facts/world of values

As British Christians we live in a society where Christianity is tolerated and even sometimes encouraged, as one among the variety of religious practices available for that minority which is 'religious'. It belongs to the private sector. Our public life, on the other hand, is governed by a different set of beliefs. Christianity belongs to the world of what we call 'values', and in this area we accept the principle of pluralism. Everyone has the right to choose the values, the lifestyle, the religious or non-religious orientation which he or she finds suitable. No one has the right to judge another in this matter. We do not use words like 'true' and 'false' in respect of these matters. They are for personal choice. The individual in his or her sovereign autonomy is free to choose. Pluralism reigns. But this applies only to the world of what we call 'values'. There is another world where pluralism does not operate. It is the world of what we call 'facts'. It is the public world — the world of science, of education, of politics and economics. On matters of fact we do not acknowledge pluralism. About facts, you are either right or wrong. If there is a disagreement about alleged facts we do not take it as an occasion for congratulating ourselves on the fact that we live in a free society where pluralism reigns; on the contrary we argue, we design experiments, we work at our disagreements until we reach agreement.

Now my point is this: in our society the things we affirm in the Christian creed are not regarded as 'facts'. They do not belong to the core curriculum in the public schools. They belong to the private world of 'values'. That every human being is shaped by the programme encoded in the DNA molecule is a 'fact' which every student is expected to know; it is part of the public education by which citizens are equipped to enter public life. But that every human being is made to glorify God and enjoy him for ever, and that every human being must in the end appear before the judgement seat of God is not a 'fact' which forms part of the curriculum. It belongs in the private sector.

The changing historical perspective

Perhaps this dichotomy becomes clearest at the point where we ask 'How is history to be understood?' For 1,000 years from Augustine, history was taught in the schools and universities of Western Europe within the framework provided by the Bible. The Bible is, of course, essentially a cosmic history beginning with the creation of all things and ending with their consummation. History is the recording of significant happenings, and no history can be written without some initial belief about what is significant, which in turn depends upon some belief about the meaning of the story as a whole. The Bible tells history from the point of view of the belief that its meaning is to be found in those events which have their crisis point in the birth, ministry, death and resurrection of Jesus. The key figures in the story are Abraham, Moses, David, the prophets, John the Baptist, Jesus, Paul.

History as taught in our schools and universities today is based upon a different belief about the human story — the belief that it is the story of man's progressive mastery of his environment and of his own development. The climax of the story is the rise of our present Western civilization and its dissemination throughout the world. The key events are Greek science and philosophy, Roman law and politics, classical culture in its Renaissance flowering, the Industrial Revolution and the new technologies. This is the real history of the world. The other way of understanding history is relegated to what is called 'religious education', and few traces of it now remain even there. The world, the real world, is understood not in terms of the biblical story, but in terms of a quite different story. This is our public world.

Reverting to the world of facts

Reference has been made to the opinion of a Roman Catholic scholar that in the minds of many of the most devout and committed African Christians today, the ancient African world-view still remains as a deep, powerful and hidden reality, often unacknowledged, but liable in moments of crisis to take over control from the consciously held Christian beliefs, see Glasser ch 3, p 9. It is surely equally clear that in the minds of many of the most devout and committed British Christians the view of the world which is created by our entire system of public education, the view which controls all our public life, the view which claims to represent 'real hard facts' as against the 'values' of religion — this view exercises enormous power — all the greater because it is not consciously acknowledged. One can believe, love and cherish the Good News of Jesus and find in it the source of peace and comfort and joy, and yet — in moments of decision — remain under the power of the dominant public world-view, the view that reality is what our science and technology tell us about 'the real facts'.

I think that the relevance of my illustration from the Ramakrishna Mission will now be clear. Multiplying pictures of Jesus in the halls of the Ramakrishna Mission while the underlying world-view remains unchallenged is not the conversion of India. Multiplying examples of personal Christian religious experience is not the conversion of England if the underlying world-view is not challenged, if Christians see their beliefs as something which belong to their private lives, while the 'real world', the world of 'hard facts' is seen in the way that our society sees it — namely as a world without God. Conversion in the fully biblical sense must mean that we find in the gospel (that is to say in the fact that the kingship of God is present in Jesus) not only a source of comfort and hope for personal living, but also the truth by which every other claim to truth whatever is finally judged.

The 'Enlightenment'

What is the source of this dichotomy (the most distinctive mark of our 'modern' culture) between a public world of 'facts' and a private world of 'values'; a public world where statements are either true or false, and a private world where such language is regarded as arrogance, where we speak only of personal choice? One could obviously develop a whole series of chapters in trying to answer that question, but for our present purpose let me just say this. When the Christian vision that had controlled the public life of Europe for 1,000 years was shattered in the religious wars of the seventeenth century, Europe sought another kind of security for the human mind than that which had been offered in the gospel. It sought it in a kind of knowledge which should be clear, exact and not open to doubt. From Descartes onwards, through many twists and turns, there has been this quest — to find a kind of certainty which cannot be doubted, a kind of knowledge about which one does not say 'I believe' (as the Christian says when he affirms the basis of his certainty), but, in the cool impersonal language of the scientific text-book: 'These are the facts.' Thus the scientist came to replace the priest as the one who can mediate and interpret to us the reality of this perplexing world in which we have to live our lives. And, whatever their protestations to the contrary, the Christian churches have largely accepted this situation, glad to be able to hold at least a corner in the private sector where personal beliefs can be cherished, but leaving the public sector to the control of another world-view. By calling it 'secular' they have tried to suggest to themselves that this is not a particular world-view, but an ideologically neutral atmosphere in which all religious faiths can peacefully co-exist. They have thus hidden from themselves the fact that it embodies a whole way of understanding human life which, in the light of the gospel, we must declare false.

Developments in physics and in scientific cosmology during the present century have shown us that the attempt to separate faith as uncertain from knowledge as certain is in radical contradiction to the way in which science actually works. Faith, so far from being a second-class substitute for certain knowledge, is itself the ground of all knowledge, the starting-point from which alone the enterprise of knowing can begin. *Credo ut intelligam*, I believe in order that I may understand, is the recipe for natural science as for all other kinds of knowing. The idea that there can be a kind of knowing which can relieve me of personal responsibility for seeking, believing and holding something as the truth is simply an illusion, the product of a guilty anxiety. As Michael Polanyi has said: 'Only beliefs which can be doubted make contact with reality' — but, he insists, they *do* make contact with reality. One could put alongside that a quotation from Einstein: 'Insofar as the propositions of mathematics refer to reality they are not certain; in so far as they are certain they do not refer to reality'. We have come a long way from Descartes! The search for a kind of certainty that relieves me of responsibility for my beliefs is futile. In a very real sense, even in the world of science, we are justified by faith.

The challenge to share the good news

As I see it, there are two implications of this for our theme. The first is that it should deliver us from a kind of timidity in our evangelism which does at present seem to afflict a lot of British churchmanship. Yes, we know that the statement that Jesus is Lord absolutely and without qualification over all worlds is a statement of faith which cannot be demonstrated to those who do not believe. But that does not mean that it is just one possible option for personal choice. Every claim to know reality is a venture of faith which cannot be demonstrated in such a way as to relieve us of the responsibility for belief. The whole of modern science, which is the child of Christendom and could not have been born of any other parent, rests upon the biblical faith that God has endowed the created world with a rationality which is contingent, and therefore to be grasped not by a priori reasoning from supposed eternal principles but by patient observation and exploration. Yes, our faith can be doubted; we know that. But so can every other claim to know reality. We know that in fact it is doubted and denied, but we bear witness that it is the truth, the truth by which every other claim to truth is to be tested. We know that we are on the witness-stand and not in the Judge's seat. We do not pretend to pronounce the judgement that he alone can and will pronounce in the end. So we give our witness with modesty. But our witness is not just to our personal experience in the field of religion. It is witness to Jesus Christ, incarnate, crucified, risen and coming to judge the world. That means that it is truth for all, and so we give our witness with humility but also with boldness (the apostolic *parrhesia*).

The challenge to change whole lifestyles

The second implication is this. We have to be prepared, however difficult it may be, to spell out the implications of the lordship of Christ for all the sectors of our public life. There can be no 'no-go' areas for the reign of God. Let us be quite clear about this. When politicians rebuke churchmen for making judgements on political issues, we are not dealing with demarcation disputes between two professional guilds. We are dealing with a conflict of faiths. We are dealing with the question: Who rules?

Let me briefly illustrate my point from one area, economics (in which I happen to have had my training). The science of economics was born out of the ideology of the Enlightenment. Before that time there was no separate science of economics. The question of how men and women behave as buyers and sellers, as employers and workers, as producers and consumers, were questions about the interpretation of God's law, God's Torah; questions about the mutual responsibility of neighbours, about greed and covetousness and self-control. Human life was seen as a network of mutual responsibilities. The new science of 'Political Arithmetic' as it was first called in Sir William Petty's book of that name, deliberately set all this aside as 'speculation' and sought to frame a scientific account of human behaviour in the economic sphere based on the analogy of Newton's laws. The physical world, as seen in Newton's vision, consisted of innumerable particles of matter moving according to the operation of gravity and inertia in orbits which could be mathematically calculated. So, by analogy, the new science saw society as an innumerable collection of autonomous individuals each seeking his or her own advantage with the least expenditure of effort, interacting in a mathematically calculable way according to the operation of the universal law of self-interest. And since, in the eighteenth century, nature had replaced God as the reality with which we have to deal, and since (for a time at least) nature has inherited God's benevolent character, nature would see to it that the operation of the universal law of self-interest would produce the good of all. As so often, Alexander Pope is the spokesman of his age:

> Thus God and Nature formed the general frame,
> And bade self-love and social be the same.

Here we have Adam Smith's invisible hand already functioning! Covetousness, which the Bible and the Christian tradition had regarded as one of the seven deadly sins, and which St Paul identified with idolatry, has become the governing principle of the social order. The entire science of economics has been developed on this basis.

The point that I wish to make is this: we are not dealing here with a neutral, secular 'factual' order into which Christianity with its 'values' has no entry. We are dealing with a different faith. The entire system is based on a doctrine of human nature incompatible with the teaching of Scripture. It is a pagan ideology. When politicians rebuke bishops for expressing judgements on matters of economics because economics is about 'facts' not about religious beliefs, we ought to recognise that a missionary frontier is opening up. We are dealing with the encounter between Christian faith and a pagan belief system. And in so far as we try to live in both at the same time, we are deeply involved in syncretism.

I give this as only one example. One could take other examples from the field of education where accepted educational principles may be found to embody a doctrine of human nature based on the ideology of the Enlightenment and not on Christian faith. My concern here is not to go into the detail of these very controversial matters, but to insist that the call to conversion in Britian today must be a call to a total renewal of the mind, to that radical U-turn which alone makes it possible to believe and confess that in Jesus the reign of God is present calling for decision now, or — to put it otherwise — that Jesus is Lord and he alone.

Lessons from the USA

What is this going to involve for Christians in Britain. Let me ask you to look for a moment across the Atlantic for what happens over there has a way of shaping what later happens here. If I may be forgiven for writing in very imprecise terms, we have had the 'mainline churches', the liberal establishment, which for many decades has tried to address public issues but with diminishing effect, mainly — I think — because the evangelical and biblical content of their message has been so diluted that it was often indistinguishable from the general ideology of the Enlightenment. We have had the conservative evangelicals, including the powerful para-church organisations, passionately asserting their fidelity to biblical faith but avoiding (until very recently) judgements on public affairs. And now we have the 'new religious right', a formidable new factor rooted in the conservative evangelical groups, but mounting a vigorous invasion of the public sphere, challenging Enlightenment values right across the board, replacing the old liberal establishment as the most powerful religious voice in politics.

It will be obvious from the foregoing argument that I am bound to wel-come this challenge to the paganism that underlies many of our sup-posedly 'secular' values, and yet that I must reject absolutely the new forms of paganism embodied in the new religious right — the sacralising of American military and economic power and the absolutising of certain American cultural values. When Jeroboam undertook to establish the worship of Yahweh at Bethel and Dan in order to legitimise his rule, he set an example which has had many imitators. There is a formidable power in this amalgam of politics and religion.

If we are to avoid falling out of one kind of paganism into a worse, how can we find the way to challenge the public ideology that rules our national life in the name and the power of the gospel? How can we call for a radical repentance, a renewing of the mind which leaves no part of our life — public or private — outside of the rule of Christ, without throwing away the good gifts which we owe to the Enlightenment — the gifts of freedom of speech and conscience? Can we affirm the rule of Christ over all our national life without being sucked into the cataract of fundamen-talism which is sweeping the world from Ayatollah Khomeni to Jerry Fal-well? Can we, as churches, develop styles (not one style) of discipleship which will offer a sign and a foretaste of the kingship of God which has come into the world in the coming of Jesus, and as it will be finally manifest to every eye when he shall come again? Only as we are enabled by the working of the Holy Spirit to do this will our call to conversion be the authentic continuation of that first call of Jesus — the call to turn round and believe in the presence of the Kingdom in him.

The Holy Spirit's authentication

When the disciples asked Jesus if they could not have the Kingdom now (a longing that we all surely share), Jesus answered them with the promise of the Spirit (Acts 1:6–8). The Spirit is precisely the foretaste, the *arrabon* of the Kingdom. It is the real presence here and now in a company of people of the love and joy and peace and freedom which are the life of the Kingdom — a reality present now, but a reality which points beyond itself because it is only a foretaste, a first-fruit, the aperitif which refreshes us and at the same time sharpens our appetite for the banquet.

There is a very important point to be made here. In relation to the call to conversion there are those who say (rightly, I think) that we have often taken the call to conversion out of the context of Jesus' preaching of the Kingdom, and made it simply a call to join the Church. That is why, for example, 'conversion' has become such a bad word in India; many Hindus see it simply as the effort of one sectional religious community to strengthen itself against the others. Seen thus, conversion looks like a sectarian, selfish activity undermining the unity of the nation — a fragile unity which needs all the strength it can get. There is justice in this protest. Yet there is also danger. We must not set 'Kingdom' and 'Church' against each other. If we do, we are in danger of making our talk of the Kingdom into a mere programme analogous to any other ideological or political programme. Jesus' initial call, I have insisted, was not the launching of a programme but the announcing of a fact — the presence of the reign of God in him. So also our evangelism is properly the announcing of a fact — the presence of the reign of God in Jesus, and its presence in *foretaste* in the fellowship of those who have accepted the call to conversion. Nothing must take away from our evangelism the reality of this *given* thing — a real foretaste now of the joy of the Kingdom; only a foretaste, but a real foretaste. Without that, the joy goes out of it.

Only the Holy Spirit can bring men and women to conversion. But the Holy Spirit is present in the community of believers as the foretaste of the Kingdom. Their common life, therefore, ought to reflect — if only in foretaste — the fullness of what God's universal reign will mean. I have talked with scores of men and women who have come to faith in Christ from other faiths or no faith. I have always been struck not only by the fact that every story is different, but also by the fact that within each story there are so many different elements. I remember reading the testimonies of about 40 people who had been converted during a period of 18 months through the ministry of a small congregation in a new industrial suburb of Madras. There was an amazing variety of experiences — apparently chance meetings, scraps of conversation, dreams, a sermon heard, a tract read, a Scripture portion studied. The overwhelming impression was that conversion was a mysterious work of the Holy Spirit who in his own way, with his own strategy, was using the faithful witness of many different people in shaping their lives towards Jesus. But one thing was common to all these stories: it was the presence of a worshipping, believing, caring community of God's people, deeply involved in the concerns of its neighbourhood (in this case heavy industry), encouraging the different gifts of all the members, always ready to give an account of the hope that was in them. Where that is present, I believe that the Holy Spirit always continues to do his mysterious work of drawing men and women, by ways that he alone knows, to give their allegiance to Jesus Christ to the glory of God the Father.

6
structural considerations

JEFFREY HARRIS

We have studied the lessons to be learnt from the British church and the world church and their response to conversion. Now we look at the structures our institutional churches have built up from the first century and see how they have hindered or aided the conversion process. Rev Jeffrey Harris is a Secretary of the Home Mission Division of the Methodist Church in the UK and applies his understanding of Church Growth principles, social and behavioural sciences, and management studies to establish guidelines. He looks at the hallmarks of the Early Church and at Luke's theology of evangelism. He then outlines the strategy and structure underlying many present churches. He uses the growth of Wesleyan Methodism as an example and then outlines some guidelines on how to build structures that aid rather than hinder the strategies that the Church is called to follow.

Ten years ago I was invited by Canon John Poulton, then Secretary of the Archbishops' Council on Evangelism, to meet two Americans who were passing through London, Donald McGavran and Win Arn. It was at that meeting that I was introduced to the Church Growth movement. A little later, an American Methodist was passing through London returning to the United States from India. In conversation we found that we were kindred spirits. His name was Geo (George) Hunter III, then Professor of Evangelism at the Perkins School of Theology in Texas. He promised to send me all the Church Growth literature which should be read. He sent me about 50 books. Later, when he was head of the Church Growth unit in the Methodist Board of Discipleship, he and his colleague, Harold Bales, came to conduct a seminar on Church Growth through which the theories came into British Methodism. George Hunter helped in the revision of McGavran's *Understanding Church Growth*[1] and brought a European dimension into the revision. He and McGavran also produced the book *Church Growth Strategies that Work*.[2]

Church Growth studies have helped me to apply the insights of the social, behavioural and management sciences to the missionary and evangelistic tasks of the Church. I had been struggling towards this synthesis in my own thinking and reading, as I first researched and then tried to find an effective strategy for the work of Methodist churches in new and expanding towns, in city centres, in inner city council estates and, to a lesser extent, in suburbs, small towns and rural areas. I had recognised that the classical theological disciplines in which I was trained could not provide the clues I needed to analyse and diagnose the reasons why so many churches were ineffective in their missionary task. I was driven into reading town planning, sociology, social psychology, and above all social anthropology, and it was in these disciplines that I began to find answers to my questions. Particularly important was the concept of culture as used in social anthropology. Later I was to see the value of management studies.

The dangers of bureaucracy

I come to this chapter, therefore, not primarily as a theoretician or academic, but as one who works within the missionary structures of the Church and has responsibility within them, and longs to see our church life more effective and productive, and at the same time, aware through these various disciplines of the dangers of bureaucracy. I have long remembered a paper read at a European Methodist Consultation on Evangelism by a Finnish Methodist, Hakan Sandstrom, on the subject of his Ph D research — Revival Movements in Northern Europe.[3] He described four phases of these movements. He showed how they began as the Spirit took hold of a group of Christians and as revival began, organisation was set up to enable the work to expand. This then hardened into an authoritarian bureaucracy which led to the beginnings of disorganisation and in turn to the petering out of the revival and the disintegration of the movement. He asked how could this general trend be halted? Could bureaucracy return to a looser, more effective organisation? He thought there was no clear or definite answer, but he could not find examples of movements in which it had taken place. If we are now nearer to the answer, as I believe we are, it is due to the application of the social, behavioural and management sciences to the missionary task of the Church. This is my starting-point.

Principles of organisational structure

First, let me set down three basic principles about structures of organisations (taken from management studies). For this purpose I regard the Church as a voluntary service organisation.

First, a good organisational structure does not simply evolve. 'Left to itself, the only things which evolve in an organisation are disorder, friction and malperformance.'[4] Nor is the right structure created by a leader using his 'intuition', any more than were the Greek temples or Gothic cathedrals built by masons using their intuition. If we are to have an organisational design and structure which produces effective performance, it will emerge only as a result of thinking, systematic analysis, and a willingness to seek an effective answer to what is discerned.

Second, designing a structure cannot be the first item on the agenda; in fact it should be the last item. All the activities that must find their place in the organisation must first be identified, and they must be enabled to perform effectively. What people actually do within the organisation is not the important factor, and the structure must not be designed to allow each person to 'do his own thing'. What does matter is the contribution they make to the organisation which enables the desired result to be achieved. What must be fitted together in the best possible way are the elements which contribute to the final effective performance.

Third, structure must always follow strategy. Organisation is not simply finding a place within the system for everything that is done. Nor can a structure be prefabricated somewhere else and simply applied to an organisation. Good structure follows strategy. It is the means by which the objectives and goals of an institution are attained. The definition of objectives comes first; this provides a base-line for assessment. Next comes a strategy to achieve those objectives. This, if effective, allows work on the structure to commence. Drucker says that this is perhaps the most fruitful and new insight which is now available in the field of organisation. Objectives are defined by asking what our organisation is for. Strategy emerges when we ask what we should be doing to attain our objectives, and to which we are prepared to commit ourselves. There are usually several answers to the question 'What should we be doing?' We have to make choices, determine priorities. The effective structure is one which is designed to allow available resources to be used in the best way to obtain performance. The key factors in the structure are those which contribute to performance. The rest are simply secondary.

Luke's theology of evangelism

Using principles such as these, it is possible to study the life of the Early Church with new understanding. Modern study of Luke has suggested that Luke was a theologian primarily, and that he selected and arranged the historical material in the Gospel and Acts in accordance with a theological pattern. Hengel has shown that Acts contains the maximum amount of material that could be contained on a single papyrus scroll.[5] Luke had to select his material carefully and omit historical data he would have liked to include — but he made his choice for theological reasons.

Luke has a theology of evangelism which can be identified from the study of Acts. It can be described briefly in the following way.

Evangelism takes place within the context of the kingdom of God. At the beginning of Acts, Jesus spends the days before the Ascension talking of the Kingdom and at the end, Paul is in Rome talking to those who visited him about the Kingdom. The Christian mission therefore, is set within the context of the Kingdom.

Evangelism is effective only in the power of the Spirit. 'You shall receive power,' Jesus promised, and that promise was fulfilled at Pentecost and renewed in the lives of the believers and in the fellowship of the Church.

The essence of evangelism is witness. 'You shall be witnesses for me.' Witness will begin in Jerusalem but spread out to reach the whole world.

Witness is to Jesus — to his life, death and resurrection.

Jesus is interpreted in different ways, to different groups of people. But the aim of the interpretation is always to enable the listener to make better sense of Jesus as Lord.

The witness to Jesus was given by followers who claimed that he was Lord. And quite simply, they wanted others to have faith in the same Lord as they did. They preached with the same aim as the apostle John wrote — 'These things are written so that you may believe that Jesus is the Christ, the Son of God, and that believing you may have life in his name.'

The evangelistic work of the Early Church took place around these six theological principles. Plainly there was a great response, especially as the good news spread westward.

Hallmarks of the Early Church

Alongside this work of evangelism and witness, we see the growth of the Church. There were five hallmarks to the life of the Church, as it grew out of its roots in Judaism and was transplanted into other cultures. These are as follows.

Spirituality: the life of corporate prayer, worship, breaking of bread, private prayer, learning more about Jesus through which the truth and reality of God's presence was increasingly made real to them.

Fellowship: a factor which was new in the religious experience, but is the consequence of the work of the Spirit. Those who believed were added to the fellowship. Fellowship means mutual commitment to do the Lord's work and to seek the presence of the Kingdom. And the gifts for this task were divided among the whole fellowship by the Spirit.

A society open to people of all classes, races and cultures: it was difficult for Jews to accept *goyim* — non Jews — into the Church, but the gospel meant that in Christ there was no Jew and Gentile, male and female, bond and free. Christians are one in Christ Jesus, and the work of the Spirit continued this.

A new lifestyle: nourished in the Law, the early Christians began to work out how they should live in future as Christ's free people, with love at the centre of all they did, fulfilling the spirit of the Law, if not the letter. They had to think what it meant to be a believer in the openly permissive world of Graeco/Roman society, and to see what were its implications when persecution of Christians began under Nero.

Continuing the ministry of Jesus: Luke describes how this came home to them as Peter and John were stopped by the blind beggar at the Nicanor or Corinthian Gate of the temple. If money had been the answer to the plea of the man, they could have got some from the common fund of the believers — but it is clear that what went through Peter and John's minds was the recognition that Jesus would not simply have given money: he would have healed the man. And this was for them the crunch. 'Look at us. In the name of Jesus Christ of Nazareth, rise and walk.' And Luke sets out a number of examples to show that the activities described in the Gospel did not cease at Calvary, but were carried on in the power of the Spirit in the Early Church. Indeed, the Gospels show that Jesus prepared these disciples for this task and gave them authority to do it. 'As the Father sent me, so I send you.'

I describe these as hallmarks of the Early Church but I believe they have to be worked out in contemporary form by the Church in every age. We must not polarise the role of the Church as either primarily evangelism or service — for there are other dimensions to its life which I have set out and which are also of the *esse* of the Church.

From this it is possible to set down the objectives of the Church.

Aims and objectives

To bear witness, in the power of the Spirit, to the truth about God who is made known to us in Jesus.

To confess that Jesus is Lord and, in the power of the Spirit, to urge all who will listen to accept Jesus as Lord and Saviour.

To point to the reality and presence of the Kingdom.

To practise and teach a spiritual life through which our experience of God is deepened.

To build up fellowship within which the value of each believer is affirmed and the gifts of the Spirit are identified and used for building up the fellowship, the practice of ministry and the work of evangelism.

To be open to all people, without discrimination in terms of class, race, culture, age or sex.

To practise a lifestyle which expresses the gospel in the various situations in which we are involved in the wider world.

To continue, in ways appropriate, the ministry begun by Jesus, which has the concept of salvation at its centre.

Strategy

Beginning with these aims and objectives, it is possible to see a little of the strategy used by the Early Church to fulfil them. However, no complete description can be given because we have only very limited knowledge of the activities which led to the growth in the number of believers and so to the expansion of the Church in apostolic times. In addition, the sense of the Spirit's power and guidance in apostolic times was so overwhelming that it is not easy to discuss the concept of strategy. Within these limitations we should note the following points.

First, the importance of proclamation, centred upon Jesus' life, death and resurrection. When Jews were present, and also Greeks who were drawn to Jewish religion, the proclamation stressed that Jesus fulfilled the prophecies concerning a Messiah, and that passages in the Psalms which spoke of David as God's chosen servant also point to Jesus as the Messiah. The response required from those who came to recognise that this message was true, that Jesus was made Lord and Messiah, and that the truth of this was demonstrated by his resurrection — was repentance, baptism in the name of Jesus for forgiveness of sins, followed by the receiving of the Holy Spirit.

Second, the apostles refused to be silenced in this witness and proclamation. When punished and imprisoned, they prayed for boldness. 'Stretch out your hand to heal and perform miraculous signs and wonders through the name of your holy servant Jesus' (Acts 4:30).

Third, in the earliest phase, proclamation and teaching about Jesus was concentrated on the temple. However, as early as Acts 5:42, Luke tells us that the life of the Church was based in private homes. This recognition of the importance of the family house was of far-reaching significance, for the household was the basic unit of city life. It had a meaning which was wider than that of the modern family. Servants, slaves and other residents belonged to the house. Christians gathered in non-Christian households (Rom 16:10, 11, 14, 15) and in houses where the father was a Christian, like Philemon, while his slave, Onesimus, was not. So by concentrating on households, Christian groups were integrated into an existing network of 'face to face' relationships, both internally (other members of the household, relatives, servants) and externally (friends, acquaintances, clients). On the other hand, there was conflict between different households in a city (See I Cor 1–4 and III John). The house was the place where preaching, teaching, sharing in meals and celebration of the eucharist took place, but the rigid family hierarchical structure of which the father was the head was not followed. This illustrates the point that the Church, in making use of important elements in a culture, does not have to take it all uncritically.

This had important consequences for our discussions. When we read in the New Testament about a Jew or Gentile becoming a Christian 'with all his household' (Acts 16:15; 16:31–34; I Cor 1:16) it must be recognised that there were different levels of commitment and personal conviction within the family. In principle, but on a much larger scale, this question arose when tribes or peoples become Christians en bloc. In this situation, people may become Christian and join the Church because of social pressure, but without experiencing conversion.

Fourth, there was recognition that the proclamation of the Word was primary, and attending to the needs of believers was secondary. So even the appointment of seven men full of the Holy Spirit and of wisdom who were appointed to free the apostles from the burden of administration was short-lived, since Stephen and Philip were quickly drawn into the task of proclamation and teaching. Philip in fact seems to have been the first to baptise a Gentile — the eunuch from Ethiopia whom he met on the Gaza Road.

Fifth, there was a general recognition, based particularly on the results achieved at Antioch, but including Peter's experience with Cornelius and his household, that the Holy Spirit was being given to Gentiles on the same terms as to Jews. The problems which arose for Jewish Christians were argued out at a Council in Jerusalem, particularly concerning the authority of the Law over Gentile Christians.

Sixth, the results achieved by the Church at Antioch led them to see that it was right to release Barnabas and Saul to go further out into the Empire with the Good News of Jesus. They commissioned them for this missionary task by prayer and the laying on of hands.

Seventh, on the second missionary journey, Paul and Silas were led by the Spirit to press on and cross to Europe — to Philippi in Macedonia. Thus the gospel which conceivably might have spread eastwards to India and China, came west and was incarnate in the cultures and ideas of Greece and Rome — and this has in turn led to the growth of Christian Europe and to Western civilisation.

Finally there was a continuing task of consolidation and instruction, advice and exhortation which was exercised by Paul to the churches he had founded.

In all these factors, the strategy was formed by recognising what the Holy Spirit was doing and where he was leading. Our accounts are incomplete, and there are huge gaps in our knowledge. Who founded the churches at Rome and Alexandria? What did the other apostles like Andrew and Philip do to help spread the faith? If it is right to see Luke as a theologian writing history, we must assume that what he describes was typical of what other apostles did also.

Structure

Given some understanding of what we would now call aims and objectives and also of strategy, how far is it possible to see these shaping the emerging structures of the Church? No group can exist long without some institutional structures. The early Christian communities had very quickly to find answers to such questions as these: How are conflicts to be resolved in our fellowship, and who has the responsibility for its oversight?

The earliest conflict was about the distribution of funds at Jerusalem (Acts 6); it was a conflict about the way in which different groups in the Church were being treated. It was resolved temporarily by appointing seven helpers, so that the Twelve were not diverted from the prior task of proclamation. A more fundamental, though not unrelated question, concerned the terms upon which Gentiles could be admitted to the Church. There was 'sharp dispute and debate' over this issue at Antioch (Acts 15:2–3) and the church there arranged for Paul, Barnabas, and some others to go to Jerusalem to see the apostles and elders about this question. The apostles and elders plainly held authoritative positions in the Jerusalem congregation (Acts 15:22) and they took decisions about the terms on which Gentiles were to be admitted with the agreement of 'the whole church'.

The structural model which is described here has been identified by Edward Schillebeeckx as a 'free association', typical of the Graeco-Roman world.[6] Membership of these free associations was open to those who wished to join but there was always an initiation process. They had a democratic form of organisation, and each developed its own ways of resolving disputes. Luke's account in Acts 15 is typical of the way that they would conduct themselves.

However, deeply divisive issues affecting the whole growing Church were not likely to be settled by a single discussion at Jerusalem. Behind the immediate question of the terms upon which Gentiles could be admitted to the Church lay the deeper one of the extent to which the culture and religious life of Judaism should determine the shape and life of the Christian church. The Jerusalem church, with James as its leading figure, plainly wished it to conform to its Jewish origins. When some of James' people went from Jerusalem to Antioch after the Council and tried to insist that Jews and Gentiles should not eat together, Peter, together with a number of others including Barnabas, did as they wanted and withdrew from fellowship at the table. Paul, however, resisted their pressure, and this left him relatively isolated. This helps us to understand why Paul took Silas as his partner on his second missionary journey and not Barnabas. It was more than an argument about John Mark's reliability. Paul believed that the Church required freedom to fashion its life and structures according to the gospel and did not accept that the discussion of major issues could be dominated by its Jewish members with solutions based on the Law, because God's Holy Spirit did not seem to distinguish between Jews and Gentiles in his work of grace.

Because Paul believed that the equal relationship of Jews and Gentiles in the Church was in fact crucial for the gospel (Gal 2:15–21), he began to arrange his own missionary programme in his own distinctive way. He remained in contact with Jerusalem, and in unity with the church there, but (with his fellow workers) established a network of communication with the churches he had founded and within which they all worked. Within this network Paul exercised a unique personal authority. From his Letters, it is possible to identify his own system of doctrine, ethics and discipline, which is usually called Paulinism. Paul did not have an easy task. For example, he had to assert his authority in the church at Corinth when he believed it was threatened by the presence of Apollos, an eloquent teacher and charismatic leader who had come from Alexandria. There was also some conflict between the various 'house churches' in the seaport. A very sharp exchange of words took place, part of which is found in the two Letters to the Corinthians, before Paul's position was re-established. It is clear that apostles like Paul, and also those he called 'fellow workers', had an influence far wider than one local church, but it certainly could not be described as universal.

Local church structures

Within a local church, complementary forms of ministry were exercised by those with the appropriate gifts of the Spirit. It is not easy to reconcile the lists of ministries which are found in I Corinthians 12:28–30, Romans 12:6–8, and Ephesians 4:16. Amongst the ministries listed are apostles, prophets, teachers, miracle-workers, healers, evangelists and pastors. Many decades passed before agreed descriptions for ministers evolved, together with the areas within which their authority was recognised. It was certainly well into the second century AD before there was reasonable clarity.

The most important words for ministers are 'elder' (or *presbyter*) and 'bishop' (or *episcopos*). The word 'elder' comes from the organised life of the synagogue and was used first in Jerusalem and then in Asia Minor and Crete, where there was a significant Jewish element in the community (Acts 11:30; 15:2, 4, 6, 22; 16:4; 21:18). Later in the first century, elders were appointed in many places. Sometimes, an elder was also called bishop, without there being, as Schillebeeckx puts it, 'any perceptible difference in their application'.[7] It is possible to distinguish between them in the second century as the Church began to adopt the imperial system of organisation, and in particular the concept of a diocese.

'Diocese' comes from the classical Greek word *dioikesis*, meaning housekeeping, management or government. The related verb *dioikein* means to manage, keep house, direct or conduct the affairs of state. The word *dioikos* means a household. Given the importance of the household in the early strategy of the Church, 'diocese' was a natural word to use within the household of faith. In pre-Christian times diocese was used to define a territorial area within which imperial administration was exercised. It was, however, a term with a changing and enlarging meaning, and by the time of the Roman emperor Diocletian, ie 297 or 298 AD, it was used technically for the 12 new regions into which the Empire was divided for the purpose of civil government, as a counterbalance to the power of the four prefectures into which the 12 dioceses were grouped. At the head of each diocese was a *vicarius* of the Emperor — a term adopted by the Church for a bishop, who was *vicarius Christi*. Later the term 'vicar of Christ' was reserved solely for the Bishop of Rome. Essentially a diocese was concerned with management and government and so the term was applied to the Church. A second word was required therefore to describe the local church and so the term *paroikia* or parish, meaning the area around the household in which the church met, came into Christian usage. At first, the terms 'diocese' and 'parish' were used side by side, as was the case with 'elder' and 'bishop', but each gradually developed a precise meaning.

The role of the bishop was strengthened as the Church faced challenges from false doctrines such as Gnosticism (in the period 135–60 AD especially) and Montanism, a movement which emphasised the work of the Holy Spirit and protested against all secularising tendencies and against the growing weight of organisation in the Church, which it claimed fettered the prophetic spirit. Montanism was essentially a liberating movement, but Montanus' declaration that he was the chosen organ of the Holy Spirit, in a time when he asserted that the end of the age was fast appearing, made his acceptance by other Christians difficult.

So, in the second century emerged the monarchical episcopate, based on the belief that all genuine Christian traditions were known to the bishops who were able to trace their line of succession back to the apostles. To provide a basic summary of Christian belief, there emerged the Apostles' Creed, which in an early and rudimentary form was known in Rome in the period between 150 and 175 AD. The authority of certain apostolic writings was also recognised, certainly in the second century, and the canon of New Testament Scripture began to emerge, though it was only at the meeting of the Third Council of Carthage in AD 397 that our present New Testament canon was finally ratified.

So we begin to see the structure of the Church. The recognised bishops and dioceses represented the organisational side of the Church, and they were the guardians of the tradition set out in the Apostles' Creed and the apostolic writings. Those who did not accept this position were outside the Church. By 200 AD the Catholic Church was more or less a fact. The word 'catholic' was first used of the Church by Ignatius in his letter to the church at Smyrna about the martyrdom of Polycarp in 156 AD; it means 'universal'. It became a technical word used to describe the whole Church.

The structures of the Church, therefore, emerged for reasons associated more closely with the common life of Christians within the fellowship than they did to facilitate the carrying out of its evangelistic role. The resolution of disputes required people with authority to act. Such authority must have a proper basis and must be widely recognised. Churches needed to be related to each other within an accepted framework. Leadership must encourage Christians faced with persecution, must safeguard them against heresy. Such leadership must uphold the apostolic teaching and be tested and measured by it. This meant that whilst genuine leadership must always be concerned with commending the faith and proclaiming the lordship of Christ, the questions which required resolution were those of the institution. When the institution's life was threatened, the Church tended to respond by erecting protective walls around itself. This position can be seen most clearly set out by Cyprian who became a martyr in 258 AD when Bishop of Carthage. 'There is one God, and Christ is one, and there is one church and one episcopate founded upon the rock by the word of the Lord'[8] ... 'Whoever he may be and whatever he may be, he who is not in the church of Christ is not a

Christian[9] ... 'He can no longer have God for his Father who has not the church for his Mother'[10] ... 'There is no salvation out of the church.'[11]

Wesleyan example

It is possible to see in this study the genesis of much discussion and conflict within the Church over the centuries about its structures and whether or not they prevent or hinder the Church from carrying out its evangelistic role. Within the limits of this chapter I cannot possibly survey the whole of Christian history. May I therefore, as a Methodist, illustrate this from my own denomination?

John Wesley, son of an Anglican rector, educated at Charterhouse and Oxford, was ordained as an Anglican clergyman by Bishop Potter in 1725 at the age of 22. He served as curate to his Father, but in 1726 he was elected a Fellow of Lincoln College and returned to Oxford where he became leader of the Holy Club. There were years of meticulous, regular, devotional discipline, and the practice of good works such as prison visiting. Out of them came a positive response to the request of Dr Burton that the Wesley brothers and one or two friends from Oxford should go as missionaries to the settlers in the new colony of Georgia. John Wesley wanted to go as a missionary to the Red Indians and not the white community. When Wesley set sail from Gravesend in 1735 he wrote, 'Our aim is not to avoid want, but to save souls, to live wholly to the glory of God.'[12] But it was the behaviour of the Moravians on that journey and the failure of his ministry in Georgia that led Wesley to write on the return journey on January 8th, 1738 when 160 miles from Lands End, 'I went to America to convert the Indians, but who will convert me?'[13] 'What have I learned ... that I went to convert others and was not converted myself.'[14] He had come a long way from the Holy Club and was now ready to understand what Peter Bohler would tell him about saving faith. So Wesley came to his experience of the heart strangely warmed in the Religious Society of Aldersgate Street on May 24th, 1738. Wesley never called this a conversion experience, but it was a turning-point in his life. In April 1739 he began field preaching, and so what is now Methodism began.

These facts have not been related to beat a Wesleyan drum. They stand to illustrate the fact that the Church as an institution, with all the riches of its spirituality and institutional life, may not succeed in bringing those who are born and live within it to conversion.

Wesley was also to find that the institutional churches do not always welcome those not under their jurisdiction if they come to proclaim the gospel within their area. Bishop Butler of Bristol found the content of Wesley's preaching 'a very horrid thing' and advised him to go somewhere else. 'You are not licensed to preach in this diocese.'[15]

Wesley was a tidy man and did not like innovation, but slowly he was compelled to innovate — societies, classes, lay preaching, extempore prayer, travelling assistants, the 'rounds' which gave birth to the circuit system, and at the end, ordination of assistants for work in America and then in England. So emerged a new denomination, even though it was against Wesley's own desire — which was to remain a member of the Church of England.

To Wesley, the evangelistic work of the Church was primary. Rule 11 of his 'Twelve Rules of a Helper' reads, 'You have nothing to do but to save souls. Therefore spend and be spent in this work. And go always not to those who want you but to those who want you most. Observe, it is not your business to preach so many times, and to take care merely of this or that society, but to save as many souls as you can; to bring as many sinners as you possibly can to repentance, and with all your power, to build them up in that holiness without which they cannot see the Lord.'[16]

All this seems clear, and yet within 20 or so years of his death, Wesleyan superintendents were trying to stop Bourne and Clowes holding their camp meeting on the slopes of Mow Cop, an action which led to the formation of the Primitive Methodist connexion; and the superintendent at Macclesfield was trying to stop evangelistic work at Bolton outside that authorised by the preaching plan — which led to the formation of the Independent Methodists.

The structure of structures

We need to ask, therefore, are there insights now available to us which help us to explain why the institutional church sometimes seems not to facilitate evangelistic outreach?

First, we should note that a hierarchical structure is not one which easily gains the committed voluntary service of members in the missionary task of the Church. Hierarchies naturally want to control and direct; they find it less easy to make space for those in local churches to be responsible for new initiatives in mission. They will lay stress on programmes devised and controlled from the centre, whereas effective evangelistic work is often the result of the Spirit blowing as he wills. Sometimes a hierarchy will allow a properly constituted missionary society to engage in evangelistic work because this has a place in the structure. Occasionally a bishop will himself be convinced of the need for evangelistic outreach and will give it priority in a diocese. We can read with profit Lesslie Newbigin's account of his approach to being a bishop in his *Unfinished Agenda*,[17] but often the weight of the institution militates against this priority. And always there is reluctance to bless what they do not control.

Second, we should notice the importance of size in relation to strategy.

A diocese or district or province is a large and complex unit, and there are a limited number of aims it can reasonably attempt. There are aims which are appropriate to a large church but which are not appropriate to a small church. On the whole, very little attention has been given to this relationship between size and strategy. The tendency is to think all churches function in the same way, but there are profound differences between a person-centred church and a programme-centred church.

Third, churches are very reluctant to define their aims and objectives and to measure results. Some will argue that the goals of churches are intangible, but attendances, memberships, confirmations, responses at an evangelistic rally, level of giving, etc, are all measurable. If you can define an objective it can be measured, and measurement or monitoring helps a church to identify actions which are effective.

Fourth, left to themselves, institutions develop resistance to change. 'In a service institution particularly' says Drucker, 'yesterday's success becomes today's policy, virtue, conviction, if not holy writ, unless the institution imposes on itself the discipline of thinking through its mission.'[18] The term used by sociologists to describe this resistance to change is 'inertia', and this is always challenged by the gospel. A resolution that a church keeps a programme of activities unchanged for another year is a vote against attempting anything new. It is a positive vote against change, though few will interpret it that way.

Fifth, churches are reluctant to commit themselves fully to seek growth. They pay lip-service to it, but growth does not happen without stress and strain. Growth in a social organisation like the Church causes as much stress as it does in a biological organism. The child puts away childish things to become an adult. If you want to save your life, you must be ready to lose it. Growth comes from discontinuity. There must be change, and change is difficult for a church to handle. The ground must carefully be prepared if there is to be change.

Sixth, the agenda of all institutions tend to be filled by issues relating to the institution's own internal life, unless those in leadership insist that priority is given to the primary objectives for which it exists. It is always easier to discuss a structure than it is to plan a new evangelistic programme. This applies at every level of the Church.

Conclusion

The aims and objectives of the Church are primary. They may be stated in terms of the Great Commission of Matthew 28:16–20, or in the terms set out earlier in this chapter. They came first and must be given the primary place on the agenda. Second comes the strategy which enables them to be worked out, and the results of that strategy must be monitored for effec-

tiveness. Third comes the structure, and the structural questions.
I believe it is possible to proceed in this way, but it requires leadership that works for effectiveness. It is for this that we must always press.

Notes

1 Donald McGavran, *Understanding Church Growth* (revised edition, Eerdmans: Grand Rapids, 1980).
2 George Hunter and Donald McGavran, *Church Growth Strategies that Work* (Abingdon Press: Nashville, TN, 1980).
3 Hakan Sandstrom, *How May We Be Evangelistic in Europe?* (Methodist Home Mission Division, 1974), pp 1–3.
4 Peter Drucker, *Management* (Harper and Row: New York, 1974), p 523.
5 Martin Hengel, *Acts and the History of Earliest Christianity* (SCM Press: London, 1979), p 8.
6 Edward Schillebeeckx, *The Church with a Human Face* (SCM Press: London), pp 48–52.
7 *ibid*, p 85ff.
8 Quoted from W Walker, *A History of the Christian Church* (T and T Clark, 1947), p 70.
9 *ibid*.
10 Quoted from H Bettenson, ed, *Documents of the Christian Church* (Oxford University Press: Oxford, 1954), p 103.
11 Walker, *op cit*, p 70.
12 *The Journal of John Wesley*, vol 1 (standard edition, Epworth Press, 1938), p 109.
13 *ibid*, p 418.
14 *ibid*, p 422.
15 *ibid*, vol 3, p 237.
16 *Constitutional Discipline of the Methodist Church* (Methodist Publishing House, 1974), pp 527–28.
17 Lesslie Newbigin, *Unfinished Agenda*, (SPCK: London, 1985).
18 Drucker, *op cit*, p 158.

7
the conciliar debate
ARTHUR GLASSER

From a general chapter on church structure we turn to one particular grouping — the World Council of Churches — and trace historically the conciliar debate in the ecumenical movement since 1960.

Arthur Glasser, who has followed these developments closely over the years, shows how the World Council of Churches has responded to the concept and implications of conversion within the wider framework of ecumenism. He faithfully reports the difficulties faced in putting evangelism and conversion on the agenda of all churches, as well as the degrees of success achieved.

Any review of the subject of conversion in the conciliar movement should begin with reference to the statement issued at the founding Assembly of the World Council of Churches in Amsterdam (1948): 'The Church's witness to God's Design'. Without ambiguity it makes the clear, biblically informed affirmation that 'the purpose of God is to reconcile all men to himself and to one another in Jesus Christ his Son.' To the Church is given 'the privilege of so making Christ known to men that each is confronted with the necessity of personal decision, Yes or No.' What is involved has eternal consequences: 'The Gospel is the expression both of God's love to man, and of his claim to man's obedience ... Those who reject the love of God remain under his judgment and are in danger of sharing in the impending doom of the world that is passing away.' In this connection Amsterdam added the note of urgency: 'If the Gospel really is a matter of life and death, it seems intolerable that any human being should live out his life without ever having the chance to hear and receive.'[1]

This concern for the conversion of all people was reinforced at Amsterdam by what has come to be known as the acid test of all mission theology: 'If we hold that Christ died for all men, and that his Gospel is to be preached to all nations, the proclamation of the Gospel to Israel stands out as an absolute obligation from which the Church must not try to escape.[2] It was quite apparent that the theological climate of the Barthian movement was dominant with its threefold emphasis: the unity of the scriptural revelation, the centrality of the atonement, and the essentiality of conversion to Jesus Christ and his lordship.

We begin with Strasbourg (1960)

In this chapter we will seek to review the major elements in the ongoing debate on conversion within the World Council of Churches from 1960 to the present. We have deliberately selected the 60s as our initial data base because it was during this period that Barthian theology lost its hold on World Council of Churches leadership, and the perspectives of Bultmann and his disciples gained the centre of the stage. Their speculations promoted a further conceptualisation of the gospel that was more congenial to the growing secularisation of Western society with its loss of transcendence, its preoccupation with material concerns, and its focus on the immediate present.

Inevitably, selecting 1960 as our starting-point is rather arbitrary. As early as the International Missionary Council conference at Willingen, Germany (1952) the term 'conversion' failed to appear in any of its final reports, although one should hasten to add that upon perusing them one has a hard time believing that conversion was not in the minds of those who drafted them. Indeed, no other goal of mission was explicitly stated. In sharp contrast, in *Student World*, David Jenkins stated that 'mission is the activity of God, not the conversion of men to belief, or the recruiting of men into the ranks of the saved...'[3]

Whereas in the early months of 1960 leaders within the World Council of Churches had good reasons for believing that all was well with their growing movement, they suddenly found that new winds were blowing. 'As usual, it began with the young people.'[4] Thus Willem Visser't Hooft described the Hoekendijk uprising that unexpectedly surfaced in their midst at a conference of the World Student Christian Federation in Strasbourg. Actually, the conference was well planned around the theme, 'The Life and Mission of the Church'. But the students became increasingly impatient as one after another ecumenical leader addressed them (Barth, Kraemer, Newbigin, Niles, and Visser't Hooft). Hoekendijk captured their imagination with his strident challenge: modern man has come of age, religionless Christianity is the new name of the game. He gave the students new slogans: Karl Barth has had his day! We don't want high churchmanship! We want high worldmanship! the Church must turn towards the world and lose itself in it! The Christian must become 'the man for others'[5] There were various reasons for this revolt. In those days many were reading and becoming mesmerised by Bishop Robinson's *Honest to God* and Vahanian's *Death of God.* Furthermore, the theologies of Tillich and the Bultmannites were beginning to take hold. The Bible was but a collection of diverse and often conflicting traditions. It had neither a fundamental unity nor a single *kerygma* for all people. This being so, the Church should not contend for the essentiality of any particular component of a conversion-to-Christ experience. Let the focus of the churches be on Jesus, the unique example of sacrificial personal concern and social service. Let them unitedly follow his lead 'doing justice and loving mercy'. This is their mission now that religious pluralism has finally triumphed in the churches.

As a result a growing silence began to pervade the churches on such themes as biblical christology, mankind's estrangement from God and the Cross as substitutionary atonement. The dominant explanation for the ancient confession, 'Christ died for us,' increasingly became that he thereby challenges us to go to the same selfless end in our service for others. Gone was the apostolic understanding that Christ 'reconciled us to God by his death' (Rom 5:10).

Then came New Delhi (1961)

The Third Assembly of the World Council of Churches at New Delhi (1961) was notable for a variety of reasons. First, the integration of the International Missionary Council and the World Council of Churches was consummated. This was a necessary forward step, for it meant that the worldwide mission of the churches would no longer be the sole province of the missions, the 'para-church' structures. All churches should recongise that they are called to mission obedience. However impeccable this reasoning, the merger represented an organisational blunder of vast proportions, which few at the time foresaw. An explanation is in order.

When New Delhi's delegates ratified the merger agreement, it represented the culmination of 'an overarching *fait accompli*, which was hardly the fault of the leadership of either the International Missionary Council or World Council of Churches, and indeed was due to mission field successes ... [represented by] the rise of the younger churches.'[6] In earlier decades many national Christian councils had emerged as a result of Western mission activity. They were composed largely of the younger churches. Unfortunately, these churches had not been encouraged to develop their own mission structures or to make provision in their councils for mission agency relationships. As a result, it soon became apparent that mission agencies which earlier had been part of the International Missionary Council would from henceforth be automatically excluded from World Council of Churches involvement. Only those societies directly related to conciliar churches could participate, and their members only as church persons, not as missionaries. Several hundred other missions, because they were not church-related, were without the prospect of World Council of Churches involvement, even had they desired it.

What this all meant was that from henceforth all debate on mission matters was to be largely in the hands of those who by training, experience, and concern were not missionaries. As a result, during the 60s one heard less and less of the traditional understanding of mission: 'The concern that in places where there are no Christians there should be Christians.'[7] Ecclesiastical concerns, not reaching unreached peoples, increasingly dominated the activities of the World Council of Churches.

Second, Orthodox churches joined the World Council of Churches at New Delhi and brought to an end its distinctly Protestant character. Of course, long before 1961 Orthodox church leaders had been in conversation with the World Council of Churches and had contributed substantially to its discussions. Notable was the reception at New Delhi of a comprehensive report to which they had contributed significantly: 'Christian Witness, Proselytism and Religious Liberty in the Setting of the World Council of Churches.'[8] It should be pointed out that the impulse for launching the extensive study that produced this report came from the Orthodox who had earlier objected to the evangelistic activities of Protestant missions among their members. Whereas this report has many notable emphases, many non-conciliar evangelicals began to wonder whether its hostility to unwarranted and unethical 'proselytism' would be abused so that 'proselytism' would become a label attached to all forms of evangelism.

A further straw in the wind was the decision taken at New Delhi regarding the Jews. As early as 1923 the International Missionary Council (at Oxford) resolved that it 'would welcome and encourage conferences looking toward more effective missionary endeavour among Jews'.[9] The first two were convened in 1927 in Budapest and Warsaw. In 1930 the International Missionary Council created the Committee on the Christian Approach to the Jews and in 1931 held a conference in Atlantic City to consider 'the Christian approach to Jews in America'. The findings of these conferences are forthrightly evangelical. But at New Delhi this committee was renamed the Committee on the Church and the Jewish People. Its subsequent publications have stressed combating anti-Semitism, eliminating misinterpretations of Judaism and the Jewish people and furthering Christian-Jewish understanding and co-operation. As late as 1966 the Committee, meeting in Sweden, urged the World Council of Churches 'to call upon all Christians constantly to bear witness in love to their faith by thought, word and deed'. But the evangelisation of Jews has steadily lost ground, indeed, ever since 1931 in ecumenical circles.

On to Mexico City (1963)

It is significant that at New Delhi the constitution of the new Commission for World Mission and Evangelism clearly spelled out its aim: 'to further the proclamation to the whole world of the Gospel of Jesus Christ, to the end that all may believe in Him and be saved.'[10] Earlier Newbigin had stated: 'The missionary movement today stands in a critical situation. If we compare the mood of the present with that of earlier decades, it is difficult to escape the impression that there is today a certain hesitancy, a certain loss of momentum.'[11] Even so, prior to the first meeting of the Commission for World Mission and Evangelism after New Delhi, in Mexico City, Newbigin sought to reverse this trend in an extended article, 'The Missionary Dimension of the Ecumenical Movement'. He sought to challenge those whose view of ecumenism was limited to drawing the churches together to express before the world their essential oneness in Jesus Christ. He did this by reiterating one of the World Council of Churches' basic postulates: 'The obligation to take the Gospel to the whole world, and the obligation to draw all Christ's people together, both rest upon Christ's whole work and are indissolubly connected. Every attempt to separate these tasks violates the wholeness of Christ's ministry to the world.'[12] Taking up this challenge Newbigin then stated:

> ... the impulse to go, to reach out beyond the accustomed boundaries for the sake of witness to Him who is Lord of all, has been central to the missionary movement and must remain so in the new circumstances which integration (the International Missionary Council and World Council of Churches) will create. Among the many things which change, this must not change. If we will think for a moment of the multitudes who are out of effective earshot of the Gospel, we shall realize how absurd is the suggestion that the call to go is no less urgent than it was when Carey wrote his 'Enquiry' or when St. Paul wrote, 'How shall they hear without a preacher, and how shall men preach unless they be sent?'[13]

Unfortunately, the Mexico City gathering did not live up to these high expectations. New Delhi had set forth a different agenda with its speculation concerning a 'cosmic Christ' penetrating all cultures and religions, first articulated by Joseph Sittler and almost immediately reinforced by P D Davanadan when he asked, 'Is the preaching of the Gospel directed to the total annihilation of all other religions than Christianity?'[14] The new implication was that religious relativism was to be approved because in the end all peoples would be saved.

At Mexico City, it was Asian theologians who in their reflection on the meaning of events in their continent 'brought into the main stream of missionary thinking the conviction that God is somehow at work in the secular events of our time, beyond the bounds of the Church'.[15] The growing popularity of such perspectives made the 1961 volume, *The Theology of the Christian Mission*, rather prophetic about mission in the 60s.[16] None of the 27 contributors attempted to deal with the concept of conversion, and there were only two incidental references to it in the whole book.[17]

It is rather strange that Mexico City endorsed what an earlier International Missionary Council gathering had condemned. Jerusalem (1928) saw ominous portents in the rise of secularism throughout the world, but Mexico City welcomed it as a liberating force. The new 'in' words elevated to priority in the missionary vocabulary of Mexico City were 'dialogue' and 'Christian Presence'. Even so, the word 'conversion' appeared (once!) in the reports drafted at Mexico City, and it seemed to mean the acknowledgement that since Christ was Saviour of all, one was thereby under obligation to serve him in the world. Conversion must be defined in terms of a person's response to the needs of this world, rather than in the traditional language of turning to God in repentance and faith. The evidence of its reality must be expressed in action for social change and the advancement of human community. Suffice it to say, in the years that followed Mexico City, the debate on conversion largely turned on the danger to the Church posed by this new attitude of solidarity with the secular world.

It is rather significant that the World Council of Churches Department of Missionary Studies convened a special four-day consultation at Iberville, Quebec, on 'The Growth of the Church' that same year (1963). The initial impulse for this consultation came from Donald A McGavran and Alan R Tippett. At that time both were active members of mainline conciliar churches and both were deeply involved in calling attention to the fact that mission strategies of the 50s and 60s were notably lacking in growth emphasis. Along with delegates from all continents, they spent four days debating, then drafting, an extended statement on the growth of the Church. Strangely, this fine statement with its emphasis on the need for conversion evangelism was not published until July 1968.[18] In an earlier issue of the *International Review of Mission* (October 1965) McGavran had written an article entitled 'Wrong Strategy'.[19] The July 1968 issue reflected some of the confusion in the churches over their missionary calling. Despite the positive thrust of the Iberville document — a World Council of Churches product — the depth and thrust of the anti-church growth sentiment in the other articles is surprising. In fact, this issue of the *International Review of Mission* convinced many non-conciliar evangelicals that despite occasional fine words to the contrary found here and there in other World Council of Churches conferences in the 60s, there seemed little possibility of the ecumenical movement spearheading missionary advance in the days ahead.

Uppsala (1968) became the nadir

The Second Vatican Council (1962–65) was convened by Pope John XXIII to deal primarily with three problems: the scandal of disunity among Christians, the application to daily life of the norms of Christian morality, and the Church's diminishing missionary activity. The final documents are replete with explicitly biblical affirmations on the essentiality of conversion (eg '... men must be called to faith and conversion.'[20] One notable passage spoke of the Council's awareness 'that there still remains a gigantic missionary task for the Church to accomplish. For the gospel message has not yet been heard, or scarcely so, by two billion human beings. And their number is increasing daily ...'[21]

It was this passage that became the focal point of evangelical reaction to the preliminary documents produced by the World Council of Churches' Geneva staff in preparation for the Fourth Assembly to be convened in Uppsala, 1968. While the Roman Catholic Church was stating very forthrightly that missionary activity is concerned with 'the task of preaching the gospel and planting the church among peoples or groups who do not yet believe in Christ,' the World Council of Churches' documents spoke otherwise. The World Council of Churches' call was for 'renewal in mission', but the term mission was made to convey ideas that had little to do with the sort of evangelistic outreach that culminated in the call for conversion. The controversy that followed polarised almost totally evangelicals both within and outside conciliar churches from the World Council of Churches' hierarchy. Even though the Assembly threw out the offending draft and sought to produce a statement more representative of its churches, the damage was done. One question was widely asked in evangelical circles: 'What is Geneva trying to do with the Christian mission?'

This polarisation was further crystallised by a series of evangelical gatherings of growing size and significance that produced documents which in no uncertain terms spoke of the redemptive heart of the gospel, of Jesus' command that it be universally proclaimed and of the ultimate aim of 'making disciples' through issuing the call to conversion. In 1966 over 900 delegates from 71 countries participated in what was called The Congress on the Church's Worldwide Mission at Wheaton and drafted a lengthy declaration (20 pages). It contained the pointed statement: 'All followers of Christ must disciple their fellowmen. From this obligation there can be neither retreat nor compromise ... When we seek the conversion of unregenerate men, even though they may be attached to some church or other religion, we are fulfilling our biblical mandate.'[22] That same year

(1966) 1,200 delegates from more than 100 countries met in West Berlin and drafted another unambiguous statement: 'One Race, One Gospel, One Task'. It too underscored the Christian obligation to make the goal of the Church 'nothing short of the evangelisation of the human race in this generation, by every means God has given to the mind and will of men.'[23]

In retrospect, the debate McGavran precipitated by standing on the side of Vatican II and asking, 'Will Uppsala Betray the Two Billion?' was somewhat overdrawn. In the World Council of Churches' pre-Assembly text conversion is not only specifically mentioned but is followed with an extensive commentary (95 lines) and is described as 'a personal re-orientation toward God'. What perhaps turned off some evangelicals was the caution that 'this must not be misunderstood individualistically'. Why this caution? Most evangelicals would immediately counter with the observation that nothing is so intensely personal as being born again!

Unfortunately, the overall thrust of this document was its silence regarding the task of bringing people to faith in Christ in obedience to the Great Commission. Attempts were made by Philip Potter (Director, Department of World Mission and Evangelism) and Eugene Smith (Executive Secretary, USA — World Council of Churches) to respond to the McGavran challenge, but with little success. Their central concern was stated by Smith when he spoke of 'a deep hesitation about drawing a clear line between the two billion who do not know Christ and the many millions who bear his Name, but whose lives deny his Saviourhood and Lordship'. He added: 'There is nausea, widespread and justified, about the kind of evangelism which calls a man to an altar and tells him he has met Christ, but sends him out with segregationist racial attitudes unchallenged and unchanged.'[24]

Actually, more impressive to evangelicals were the reports of John Stott of All Souls Church, London, and David Hubbard, President of Fuller Theological Seminary. Both attended the Uppsala Assembly and both felt that even the revised section of 'Renewal in Mission' did not 'provide sufficient emphasis on world evangelism'. They found only 'rather isolated concessions to evangelical pressure'. Whereas they were deeply moved by and supportive of the Assembly's concern for 'the hunger, poverty and injustices of the contemporary world' they found 'no comparable compassion or concern for the spiritual hunger of the unevangelized millions'. They saw significance in 'the fact that the draft was altered almost beyond recognition.' This was proof 'that the pre-Assembly committee was in no way representative of the Council'. Both were baffled over 'why we had to work so hard in a Christian assembly to agree on things that are such basic Christian affirmations?'[25] The die seemed cast. On issues related to evangelism and conversion both ecumenicals and evangelicals seemed determined to move in opposite directions.

This determination seemed particularly apparent when it came to the impatience with which they reacted to the popular slogan of the 60s: 'The World Provides the Agenda.' Many evangelicals contemptuously dismissed it as absurd: imagine a sinful world in its rebellion against God telling the Church what the gospel is! And not a few ecumenicals read the slogan to mean that all activities contributing to the humanisation of society are of God, even those that are quite independent of the Christian community. The Christian mission , therefore, was to identify with these activities and support them in collaboration with God. We rejoice that this deliberate misrepresentation of the Church's task was challenged by John V Taylor — a prominent ecumenist — with the necessary witness that this implied that 'if he chose, God might have accomplished the renewal of man without Jesus Christ'.[26]

Of course, what the slogan meant was that the Church must take seriously the concerns of the world and address these concerns in its proclamation of the gospel. Had evangelicals been more involved in the ecumenical debate instead of firing long-range blasts against everything emanating from Geneva, they might have said: 'Yes, we should not abruptly tell the world that its concerns are of no consequence and that it should listen to the real concerns of the Bible. We should rather accept their concerns, and then address them to the Bible, so that answers are forthcoming that express the gospel in terms of their agenda.' If Calvin said that the spectacles of Scripture were needed to discern the embodiment of divine thought in the phenomena of nature, the constitution of the human mind, and in human experience, surely Scripture reveals its truth more clearly to those who are sensitive to the insights and concerns of people today. Special revelation (the Scripture) has its contribution to general revelation and vice versa. The agenda of the world provides us with questions to address Scripture. Only when the Word of God is studied in the arena of today's public debate will its full measure of the gospel be heard. It is greatly to be regretted that in the strident polarisations of the 60s both evangelicals and conciliars managed to impoverish themselves. Few had a comprehensive biblical word for a terribly confused decade.

Improvement in the 1970s

At first, the polarisation seemed to deepen. Peter Beyerhaus was instrumental in convincing a sizable number of German theologians and church leaders — all with impeccable intellectual credentials — to draft what came to be known as the Frankfurt Declaration. This was a straightforward though hard-line exposure of the World Council of Churches' reduction of the Christian mission to secular humanism. Then came the 'Salvation Today' Assembly of the Department of World Mission and Evangelism at Bangkok in 1972/73. Its pre-conference literature gloried in religious relativism. The Geneva staff that prepared it seemed oblivious of the growing groundswell of evangelical impatience with the World Council of Churches. There were stories of being saved by Mao alongside being saved by Jesus, the approval of the World Council of Churches being given to a priest apostasising in Japan, and the pouring of religious significance into the nationalist feelings of an Israeli Jew in the 1967 Six Day War. All this under such questionable statements as: 'A fuller understanding of the contemporary meaning of salvation requires a better practice of dialogue between people of different faiths' or 'religious fellowship within the Church and the human fellowship in secular society are both created by the Gospel and are within the reality of Christ and the history of salvation in the world'.[27]

Evangelicals expected no good to come out of Bangkok. Those who attended were confirmed in their darkest thoughts when they heard the director of the one unit within the World Council of Churches devoted to 'world mission and evangelism' open the conference with the irresponsible, unbiblical statement that all talk about the two billion without Christ was 'totally futile'.[28] Surprise of surprises, when the conference ended it became apparent that the delegates had challenged these Geneva perspectives. Even so there was much incomprehensible mixture in the final documents.

Having said this, it should be noted that Bangkok said more on the subject of conversion than any previous ecumenical gathering. Acts 4:12 was included without comment, but the delegates after six separate attempts found that they could not agree on a definition of the uniqueness of Christian conversion as against conversion in other religions. Once again evangelicals struggled to get the Assembly to be more straightforward in its biblical confession. They suggested a comprehensive imperative, but it only barely passed: 'Each generation must evangelize its own generation. To work for church growth and renewal is the chief abiding and irreplaceable task of Christian mission.' A final statement 'imploring' men to accept God's salvation in Jesus Christ was also almost struck out as 'irrelevant'.[29]

Then came Lausanne 1974: The International Congress on World Evangelization. *Time* magazine described it as 'a formidable forum, possibly the widest-ranging meeting of Christians ever held'. It brought together 2,473 evangelical leaders from 150 countries and 135 Protestant denominations. Its theme was 'Let the Earth Hear His Voice.' Its culmination was the release of *The Lausanne Covenant*, a comprehensive statement on mission and conversion evangelism that rapidly became the rallying point of evangelicals around the world, both within and without the conciliar movement. This document is built around a biblical theology of conversion that demands missionary obedience. Lausanne was not only an 'event'. It initiated an 'ongoing process' of regional conferences, study commissions, and publication programmes that has continued to the present without abatement. Suffice it to say, Lausanne gave evangelicals such an international corporate prominence and recognition that conciliars feared it would precipitate the emergence of a rival to the World Council of Churches. Fortunately, evangelical leaders in their shared burden for renewal within existing churches have eschewed all desire to compete with the World Council of Churches through establishing a parallel council of churches. Actually a large number belong to the World Council of Churches' member churches and find no biblical warrant for competing with them in such a fashion.

It is rather significant that when Lewis Smedes of the Fuller Theological Seminary faculty participated in a gathering of The Faith and Order Commission of the World Council of Churches in Accra (1974), he was surprised by what he encountered: not only that 200 theologians from diverse church traditions engaged in hard, patient, candid dialogue, but also their awareness of the theological implications of Lausanne and their 'genuine wish to listen to the message of Lausanne, to listen and to let it teach'. One study group spent two full mornings discussing the Wheaton Declaration (see p 90). And he found 'no inclination to trade in the Christian hope for a mess of political pottage'.[30] Obviously, there is more to the World Council of Churches than that dominant segment which would radicalise the Christian mission. Smedes' closing comment is significant:

I was impressed by both the seriousness in which the conference confronted some of today's most nettlesome issues and its openness to minority viewpoints. I was limited in my participation, for instance, only by my own resources and abilities. Once in the swing of things, anyone can be as influential as anyone else. My own role in Faith and Order was an *ad hoc*, one-time thing. It is unfortunate that evangelicals do not have an ongoing share. For whatever else Faith and Order is, it is an open consultation. Obviously, Faith and Order is not identical with the World Council; what bearing the Accra discussions will have on the next General Assembly in Nairobi is anybody's guess. But whatever the visible outcome, Faith and Order in my judgment deserves the best contribution evangelicals could make it — not because of what it has accomplished, but because of what it tries.[31]

Will there be convergence?

Then came Nairobi 1975. At this Fourth World Council of Churches Assembly the ecumenical movement seemed to be turning a corner. The theme was 'Jesus Frees and Unites.' When Bishop Stephen Neill reviewed the preliminary documents, he could not but describe them as 'not encouraging ... very uneven ... few qualify as serious statements ... unbelievable triviality,' etc. He concluded: 'Unless the Holy Spirit is very notably at work during the period which remains for preparation, and in the proceedings of the Assembly itself, Nairobi 1975 might well be the last Assembly of the World Council of Churches.'[32] Professor Meyendorff, the most popular spokesperson for Orthodoxy, expressed the hope that 'an Orthodox contribution to the discussion in Nairobi may contribute to salvaging [the Ecumenical Movement] at a time when so many people, both inside the Orthodox Church and outside it, have lost confidence in Ecumenism'.[33]

Despite the fact that Philip Potter had told the Synod of Catholic Bishops in Rome (1974) that the ecumenical theme *par excellence* of the World Council of Churches was evangelisation, his report to the Nairobi Assembly made no mention of it. His preoccupation was with the struggle for social justice and the humanisation of society. Even so, the Assembly chose to emphasise evangelism. Most of the delegates wanted to participate in the discussion on 'Confessing Christ Today', and they produced an excellent statement that did not merely stress confessing Christ as Saviour and Lord but emphasised 'Confessing Christ as an Act of Conversion'. In many ways the references to conversion were similar to those in the Lausanne Covenant. Indeed, some of the basic charges of evangelicals against the position of the World Council of Churches on evangelism were no longer valid.

Then followed the Commission for World Mission and Evangelism gathering at Melbourne (1980) under the rubric 'Your Kingdom Come.' It was followed five weeks later by a Lausanne-oriented Consultation on World Evangelisation convened at Pattaya, Thailand. It divided the human race into 17 distinct units and assigned groups to grapple with the theme, 'How Shall They Hear?' Melbourne began to reflect some of the Faith and Order-sponsored studies on conversion (not before 1963) that had not impacted on previous World Council of Churches or Commission for World Mission and Evangelism gatherings.

It should be noted that in 1967 a whole issue of *The Ecumenical Review* was devoted to the theme of conversion, and Paul Loffler of the Department of World Mission and Evangelism during the 60s became known for his writings on conversion — but all this failed earlier to gain the attention it warranted.

It was at Melbourne (1980) that Emilio Castro, the leader of the Department of World Mission and Evangelism, contended courageously for conversion evangelism. He also addressed the delegates at Pattaya. Evangelicals were not very gentle with him in the discussion that followed, and pressed him hard on whether he was infected with the universalist heresy that made conversion irrelevant. Few realised that he was then deeply involved in a comprehensive study on evangelism in which he invited key evangelicals to participate. The result was an illuminating and thoroughly evangelical document, *Mission and Evangelism: An Ecumenical Affirmation.* The Central Committee of the World Council of Churches received and approved it in 1982. At long last evangelicals felt that the Department of World Mission and Evangelism's understanding of conversion was being shaped by Scripture and expressed in ways consonant with the intimate relation between conversion and 'doing justice and loving mercy' (after the pattern of Amos 5:15 and Matthew 23:23).

Then came the Sixth Assembly at Vancouver (1983). The dominance of Philip Potter was painfully felt by evangelicals at the outset when he and all other plenary speakers failed even to mention the Affirmation. Was the World Council of Churches still in the trough of the 60s? Apparently not! The Affirmation received strong support in the 'Program Guidelines Committee Report', in other reports, and in the Assembly's 'Message to the Churches'. When later Emilio Castro was appointed to the leadership of the World Council of Churches, many felt that an old order had passed away and that a new one was emerging. But of this, only time will tell. Suffice it to say, evangelicals will never retreat from either gospel proclamation or the invitational dimensions of evangelism.

Notes

1 *Man's Disorder and God's Design,* Amsterdam Assembly Series vol 2 (Harper and Brothers: New York, 1948), pp 212, 217.
2 *ibid,* p 168.
3 David Jenkins, 'The Church, Bride of Christ, and her Mission', *Student World,* vol 50, no 1 (1957): p 336.
4 Willem Visser't Hooft, *Has the Ecumenical Movement a Future?* (John Knox Press: Atlanta, 1976), pp 24–26.
5 *ibid,* pp 24–26.
6 Ralph Winter, 'Ghana: Preparation for Marriage', *International Review of Mission,* vol 67, no 267 (1978): p 344.
7 Lesslie Newbigin, 'Mission and Missions', *Christianity Today,* vol 4, no 22 (August 1, 1960): p 911.
8 'Christian Witness, Proselytism and Religious Liberty in the Setting of the World Council of Churches', *Evanston to New Delhi* appendix 8 (World Council of Churches: Geneva, 1961), pp 239–45.
9 William Richey Hogg, *Ecumenical Foundations* (Harper and Brothers: New York, 1952), p 238.
10 Quoted in 'Mission to Six Continents', Harold E Fey, ed, *A History of the Ecumenical Movement,* vol 2 (Westminster Press: Philadelphia, 1970), p 190.
11 Lesslie Newbigin, 'One Body, One Gospel, One World', *The Ecumenical Review,* vol 11, no 2 (January 1959): pp 143–56.

12 Lesslie Newbigin, 'The Missionary Dimension of the Ecumenical Movement', *The Ecumenical Review*, vol 14, no 2 (January 1962): pp 207–15.

13 *ibid*, pp 212, 213.

14 Joseph A Sitler, 'Called to Unity', *The Ecumenical Review*, vol 14, no 2 (January 1962): pp 177–87; Paul D Devanadan, 'Called to Witness', *The Ecumenical Review*, vol 14, no 2 (January 1962): pp 154–63.

15 'Mission to Six Continents', Fey, *op cit*, p 194.

16 Gerald Anderson, ed, *The Theology of Christian Mission* (SCM Press: London, 1961).

17 Eric J Sharpe, 'The Problem of Conversion in Recent Missionary Thought', *The Evangelical Quarterly*, vol 41, no 4 (1969): p 221.

18 See studies of Church Growth in *International Review of Mission*, vol 57, no 227.

19 Donald A McGavran, 'Wrong Strategy', *International Review of Mission* (October 1965): pp 451–61.

20 Vatican II Documents: *Constitution on the Sacred Liturgy (Sacrosanctum concilium)* 9; *Decree on the Church's Missionary Activity (Ad gentes)* 7, 13, 40; *Decree on the Ministry and Life of Priests (Presbyterorum ordinis)* 4, 18; *Decree on Ecumenism (Unitatis redintegratio)* 7, 8; etc.

21 *Decree on the Church's Missionary Activity (Ad gentes)* 10.

22 Harold Lindsell, *The Church's Worldwide Mission* (Word Books: Waco, Texas, 1966), p 226.

23 Carl F H Henry and W Stanley Mooneyham, *One Race, One Gospel, One Task*, vol 1 (Worldwide Publications: Minneapolis, 1967), p 5.

24 Eugene L Smith, 'Renewal in Mission', *Church Growth Bulletin*, vol 5, no 2 (November 1968): pp 325, 326.

25 John R W Stott and David Hubbard, 'Does Section Two Provide Sufficient Emphasis on World Evangelism?', *Church Growth Bulletin*, vol 4, no 2 (November 1968): pp 329–33; 'The Theology of Section Two', *Church Growth Bulletin*, vol 4, no 2 (November 1968).

26 *Uppsala Report* (World Council of Churches: Geneva, 1968), p 23.

27 *Salvation Today and Contemporary Experience* (World Council of Churches: Geneva, 1973), pp 37, 39, 106–7, 103–4, 4.

28 Philip Potter, 'Christ's Mission and Ours in Today's World', *Bangkok Assembly 1973* (World Council of Churches: Geneva), pp 51–63.

29 Ralph Winter, *The Evangelical Response to Bangkok* (William Carey Library: Pasadena, 1973), p 102; McGavran, *op cit*, p 303.

30 Lewis B Smedes, 'Christian Hope at Accra', *The Reformed Journal* (November 1974): p 17.

31 *ibid*, p 20.

32 Stephen Neill, 'The Nature of Salvation', *The Churchman*, vol 89 (July–September 1975): pp 225–34.

33 Ian Bria, 'Confessing Christ Today', *International Review of Mission*, vol 64, no 253 (January 1975): pp 70, 71.

8
a measure of his purpose
PETER BRIERLEY

No study of conversion would be complete without some of the statistical evidence gathered over the years. Man is always attempting to measure different aspects of the Christian faith, and this activity is sometimes more effective if it involves quantitative rather than solely qualitative aspects.

Peter Brierley, now European Director of MARC Europe, has been researching Christian events and trends for nearly 20 years. He worked formerly with the Bible Society. In this chapter he studies in depth the 1968 survey on conversion. He concludes with a listing of the various factors that brought many famous people to conversion.

To understand God's thoughts we must study statistics, for these are a measure of His purpose. (Florence Nightingale)

Introduction

Earlier chapters in this book have focused on the quality and motivation of conversion. These aspects are vital to our understanding of the subject, but we cannot neglect to look at numerical facts. Little study of this nature has been done; nevertheless, this chapter seeks to explore the significance of the reliable surveys that are available.

A survey on conversion was carried out to aid the Commission on Evangelism set up by the Evangelical Alliance in 1967. The full Commission Report was published with the title *On the Other Side*. The survey itself was also published by Scripture Union in 1968 under the title *Background to the Task*. Regrettably, this 20-year-old survey is the only such study known to have been carried out in this way. Since no more up-to-date data exists, perhaps future study should be commissioned to look at factors behind conversion in the 1980s.

Five thousand questionnaires were distributed through clergy associated with the Evangelical Alliance. These were therefore evangelical Christians. The sample was balanced by age and sex with the general population, but there were more middle-class respondents than in the population as a whole. The response rate was 80%, giving the study a basis for reliable results.

Certainty of conversion

The survey showed that 67% knew the exact day they were converted. Obviously that means 33% did not know the precise day, even though they were certain they were Christians.

How has that figure varied with time? Over the 50 years following the end of the First World War (1918–68) the proportion of evangelicals knowing exactly when they were converted has hardly varied from the 65–70% range. The only significant variation was after Billy Graham's 1954 Harringay Crusade when the proportion rose to 75%. Prior to the First World War, however, the proportion was lower — on average 55%, but fluctuating between 45% and 65%. This might be due to a changing pattern of emphasis, or may just reflect that people could not remember when asked about an event — albeit a very personal and profound event — 50 years or more ago.

Factors leading to conversion

Given reliable statistics and the certainty of those who participated in the survey that they had indeed been converted, it is worth asking how that conversion took place. The largest group were converted through the activities of their local church. This accounted for 3 people in every 10. Occasional activities, like camps, or missions, or other one-off events, helped a further 2 in 10 to find Christ. Personal witness accounted for a further 15%. Large-scale meetings with a professional evangelist had helped one person in eight to become a Christian. Half the remaining 22% had come to faith through the regular youth work of the church (including the Sunday school), and the rest through reading the Scriptures, or seeing a film or listening to the radio or reading a Christian book. (See Chapter 11 of this book for a graphical analysis.)

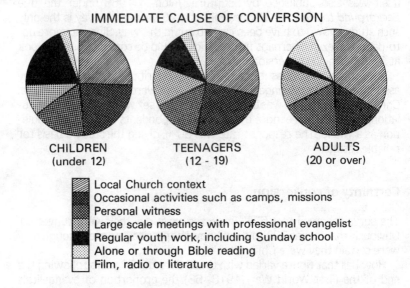

IMMEDIATE CAUSE OF CONVERSION

CHILDREN   TEENAGERS   ADULTS
(under 12)   (12 - 19)   (20 or over)

Local Church context
Occasional activities such as camps, missions
Personal witness
Large scale meetings with professional evangelist
Regular youth work, including Sunday school
Alone or through Bible reading
Film, radio or literature

Figure 1

More information is revealed when the converted are broken down by age groups, as Figure 1 illustrates.

Children and teenagers are more likely to find Christ at camps and missions. Their work is obviously most important. Likewise regular youth work and Sunday school is more important the younger people are. Professional evangelism, on the other hand, is more relevant for teenagers and adults (as Mission England and Mission to London have more recently confirmed). Church involvement becomes the dominating factor for adults though personal witness is also a large component. Married people come to Christ largely in a local church context, through personal witness or through the reading of the Scriptures. How have these various factors varied over the last 70 years? Let us take those converted through the outreach of the local church. The proportion thus converted is given in Figure 2.

Those who found Christ between 1904 and 1908 through their church were about 45% of all who had a definite conversion in those years. In the next five years, 1909–13, this proportion fell to 35%, and over the First World War, 1914–18, it fell again to 27%. In the 1919–23 period, however, it rose again to nearly 45% and then in the next two five-year periods successively dropped, only to rise again to over 40% between 1934 and 1938. The graph shows these 15-year cycles very clearly. Only in recent times, with the many conversions through the Harringay and

DEFINITE CONVERSIONS
IN A
CHURCH CONTEXT

DEFINITE CONVERSIONS
THROUGH A
PROFESSIONAL EVANGELIST

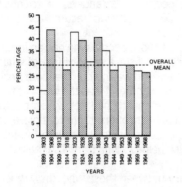

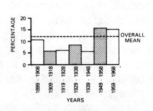

Figure 2   Figure 3

Wembley Crusades, has the pattern been modified. How it has continued since 1968 is not known; a new study would need to be undertaken. Why this pattern? Do churches need time to consolidate after times of an influx of new members? Or does the excitement of outreach pale until a new generation arises or a new minister comes? Unfortunately the reasons were not probed in this survey.

Let us look next at definite conversions through a professional evangelist. This is graphed in Figure 3 in ten-year periods.

The Billy Graham Crusades of 1954, 1955, and 1967 produce a definite hump in the graph. There is also a high peak in the graph at the beginning of the century and in the 1930s. What evangelists were there then? The Welsh revival occurred in the first period, and Tom Rees was very active in the second.

Influences leading to conversion

We have looked thus far at the immediate cause of a person's conversion, according to self-assessment. What likewise were the factors which led up to that moment of conversion? What were the essential influences at work? The most important was the influence of the home — the Christian home — and the witness of relatives. These helped many people come to faith because they saw Christianity being lived out.

The next factor, almost equal in importance, is personal witness outside the home. The imperative of sharing one's faith with other people is clearly seen. Even if ultimately the actual cause of conversion is not leading somebody to Christ, a person's witness often influences people, and often this is unrealised. Who are these outside people — strangers, or friends? Unfortunately this was not probed. But these two factors together account for three-fifths of all conversions.

The remaining two-fifths is made up of those people who had an internal feeling or compulsion, such as conviction of sin, a sense of fear of what might happen, or not knowing where the world was going. Their worry or concern helped them to come to Christ. Sometimes it was the work of the local church; perhaps actual attendance at church had helped people to realise their need of faith but hadn't actually brought them to a place of conversion. Christian teaching among youth outside the church (and so almost certainly in a school context) also helped some to realise the truth of Christianity.

How do these various influences vary between those who knew when they were converted (for simplicity let us call these 'definite' conversions) and those who whilst sure they were Christians were not sure exactly when they came to know the Lord (let us call these 'indefinite' conversions)? Those with definite conversions were more influenced by personal witness *outside* the home, and by personal, internal feelings; external factors to their home community or deeply private concerns were more important here. Those with indefinite conversions found the home and the witness of relatives more important, and also the general background of the local church; these latter factors suggest a warmth of security and acceptance and a gradual coming to faith in such a caring context. How have these influences varied over time?

Figure 4 shows definite conversions influenced by the witness at home or by relatives, since the beginning of the century — no neat 15-year cycles here! What clearly emerges is the huge drop in the influence of the home across the years. Where is the Christian home influence? It is declining, and the graph captures that drop, and the sorrow of it. We are losing ground in the home.

On the other hand, Figure 5 shows the influence of personal witness outside the home, which is clearly increasing. Sharing the faith is becoming, as it were, more crucial. The lifestyle of people in their particular work or social context becomes important. The living out of the life of Christ bears its own testimony.

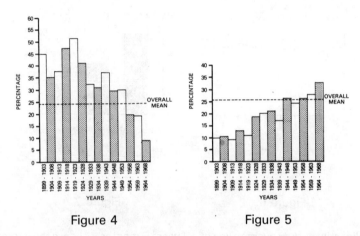

DEFINITE CONVERSIONS
INFLUENCED BY
HOME WITNESS OR RELATIVE

DEFINITE CONVERSIONS
INFLUENCED BY
PERSONAL WITNESS OUTSIDE THE HOME

Figure 4   Figure 5

Sex of those converted

The survey showed that of every 20 men who were converted, 9 went to church regularly before their conversion. Of every 20 women who were converted, 11 went to church regularly. so there is more church-going by women, and it seems to have a greater effect on a woman.

Age of conversion

The survey showed 17% of the sample was converted when under 12 years of age. A further 59% were converted in their teenage years, 12–19, leaving 24% who were converted as adults. Now those figures — based on 4,000 people — are significant. Three-quarters found Christ before they were 20. The actual average age was 14 years 9 months. The average was slightly rising over the 1960s, as Figure 6 shows. It would be interesting to know whether it had continued to rise in the 70s and 80s.

The average age for a man finding Christ was 15 years, but the average age for women was 14 years 7 months. Women come to faith earlier than men. Why? Those who come from a Christian home were converted

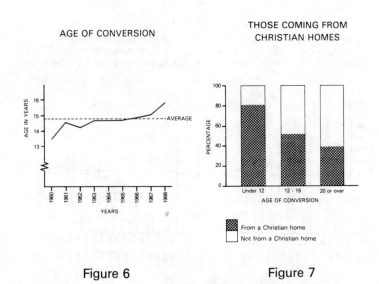

Figure 6   Figure 7

earlier still — at an average age of 14 years 5 months — hence the importance of a Christian home. Those who could say they had a definite experience of conversion were converted on average at a slightly higher age than
the others: 14 years 11 months.

Figure 7 shows those people who were converted who came from a
Christian home. Four-fifths of children finding Christ came from a Christian home. Just over 50% of teenagers coming to faith came from a Christian home, but under 40% of converted adults came from a Christian
home. The particular importance of our homes comes out in this simple
graph. The graph also shows that if only 20% of children finding Christ
come from *outside* Christian homes, we may be insularising ourselves as
a Christian community — not reaching out effectively enough.

Let us look now at people converted who actually went to church before
their conversion. Figure 8 shows the proportion of those aged under 25,
and Figure 9 those aged 25–34.

Two things emerge from these graphs. The Church exercises a declining
influence on young people; it has broadly and uniformly decreased since
1950, particularly among those aged 25–34. This is a tragic fact, because
these are potential leaders. The graph reflects those who have, in fact, sub-
sequently been converted. But what of those who were influenced less and
have now left the Church?

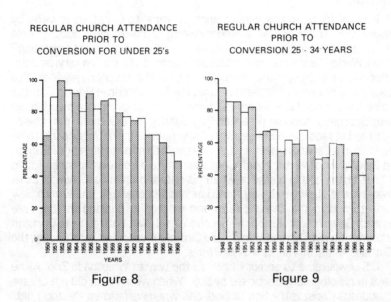

REGULAR CHURCH ATTENDANCE
PRIOR TO
CONVERSION FOR UNDER 25's

REGULAR CHURCH ATTENDANCE
PRIOR TO
CONVERSION 25 - 34 YEARS

Figure 8

Figure 9

Testimonies of conversion

It is fascinating to look at how some of our church leaders have been converted through visions like St Paul, or the Emperor Constantine, or Ignatius Loyola, the founder of the Jesuits. So was Blaise Pascal, the scientist/mathematician; George Fox, the leader of the Quakers, and David Brainerd, the missionary to the American Indians. Sojourner Truth, the emancipated Dutch slave who was involved in desegregation, early found Christ through a vision. Leo Tolstoy would say he was converted by a vision of Christ. Malcolm Muggeridge would put down his conversion to a vision, as would Claire Luce, the Catholic editor of *Life* and *Vogue* magazines. People who have had visions have lived in all centuries, but that's only one way of coming to Christ.

Reading the Bible is another. Augustine read the Bible and was converted. So did Calvin, and John Bunyan. So did Jonathan Edwards, the preacher, and Charles Finney, the revivalist. Likewise the Christian biographer, C F Andrews, and Eldridge Cleaver, the leader of the Black Panther militant group.

Others have been converted through reading a Christian book. Teresa of Avila, the Roman Catholic Carmelite nun, found Christ that way. So did

Charles Colson, who read a book by C S Lewis. How else have people come to Christ? George Whitefield came through fasting. Peter Cartwright, the American Methodist politician, through fear of death.

Each of these, in one way or another, came to Christ, as it were, by themselves. Other people were not directly involved. What about people when other people were involved, as in a church service, or a meeting? John Wesley found his heart strangely warmed in a church service. John Woolman, the Quaker, and Barton Stone, the Presbyterian revivalist, also thus came to Christ. Elizabeth Seaton, the first American Roman Catholic saint, who started the Sisters of Charity, was converted in a meeting. So was Spurgeon, and the preacher Billy Sunday. W T Grenfell, the missionary to Labrador, and Stanley Jones, the famous Indian missonary, came to faith in a Christian meeting. Lin Yu Tang, a Chinese professor of English in Peking, who went through Confucianism to become a Christian, found Christ at the end in a service when his wife took him to a church. Ethel Waters, the black Broadway musician, and Simone Weil, the French Jew who turned to the Catholic faith and worked in England for the Free French Government during the Second World War, both came to Christ in a church. So did Thomas Merton, the Catholic mystic, and John Cogley, the Catholic editor of *The New York Times*.

C S Lewis came to accept Christ on the way to Whipsnade Zoo. As he says in his biography *Surprised by Joy*: 'When we set out I did not believe that Jesus Christ is the Son of God, and when we reached the zoo I did.' Some journey!

With a sense of service, Albert Schweitzer, feeling desperately concerned to reach people in Africa, came back and started to train as a doctor when he was 40. That was his motive, and he would say it led to his conversion.

Many prominent Christian leaders have come to faith through their home as a child. David Livingstone did, as did William Booth, the founder of the Salvation Army. Likewise Francis Thompson, of the 'Hound of Heaven' fame. For Sergius Bulgakov, the Eastern Orthodox Dean of the French Orthodox Academy, and Evelyn Underhill, the Anglican mystic, it was their home which was crucial. Samuel Shoemaker, the dynamic Episcopal preacher in America, and Dorothy Day, the leftist Catholic author both took their initial steps to faith as a child. Evelyn Waugh, the novelist, and Dag Hammerskjöld, twice-elected Secretary-General of the United Nations, both looked to their homes as the place where they found Christ.

These brief glimpses of history show that God uses different circumstances in a wide variety of ways. Some are fairly recent. Others span the centuries. God works in a mysterious way!

Conclusion

What is the overall picture? What are the key factors in conversion? The age of those going to church is a major element. We have massive numbers of boys and girls in our churches; 35%, a third of all those who come to church, are under 20. We have more children in our churches than the proportion in the population would expect us to have. It is this group whose response stands out so starkly from the survey on conversion. Thus it is crucial to reach young people.

Second, personal witness, especially to those outside the home, is important. At a survey of those attending All Souls Church in London, almost half went because of the church's reputation, and about a third through personal invitation. But of those who weren't Christians before they went, two-thirds went because of a personal invitation. Hence the importance of friendships as a basis for personal work.

Third, the Christian home is a crucial influence. There is nothing quite like it! Hence the importance of reaching families for Christ, of reaching men and women in their early twenties who will be starting homes and families when they are married. Let us never underrate the impact of a Christian heritage reflected in the earliest memories of a child.

9
the role of the local church

MICHAEL WOODERSON

The 1968 survey showed that roughly 30% of those professing conversion did so in a church context. The lessons learned from the 1983/84 Missions showed the importance of the local church not only as the nursery for new converts but also of their missionary orientation. If the local church is to be effective in its outreach, it needs training: Michael Wooderson describes a scheme which mobilises the whole congregation for effective evangelism and church growth. His Grove Booklet Good News Down the Street *was born out of his experience as District Minister of St Thomas, Aldridge. He is now Vicar of Chasetown, in Staffordshire.*

This practical chapter outlines the problems of conversion in the traditional church as well as the expectations of leadership and congregation. He provides notes on Body training and shows how churches can respond to the opportunities that come to them.

The starting-points

Conversion is ultimately a 'mystery'. The psychological processes are often hidden and subtle, and not everyone can describe them with certainty or accuracy, nor should they be expected to. This is particularly the case for those who have grown up in a Christian household and grown into the Christian faith without undergoing a clear-cut conversion experience. There is no doubt that they have personally appropriated the salvation won for mankind by the death of Christ on the cross. There is ample evidence of their deep and ongoing discipleship. Much Anglican church life has been built around the assumption that this process of gradual absorption into the fellowship of the church is the normal and proper way of entry into Christian discipleship.

From such a standpoint conversion — as in St Paul, the conversion of — can be a source of embarrassment. A conversion of that nature strikes a discordant note; it makes others feel uncomfortable, or even threatened, because it is alien to their experience. New converts may also express their faith with rather more emotion and exuberance than is common among church-going people, and their enthusiasm for their new-found faith can be a trifle unsettling. Conversion, therefore, is often regarded with suspicion or even hostility in certain quarters; it is relegated to the outer fringes of the church and left to the 'sects' or the fanatics, the Pentecostals or the evangelicals. Yet conversion was at the very heart of New Testament Christianity, and every local church needs to come to terms with its importance, not least because we find ourselves on a mission field today in this country.

The possibilities

Karl Rahner, taking a prophetic look at the Roman Catholic Church in Europe in his book *The Shape of the Church to Come*, wrote: 'The possibility of winning new Christians from a milieu that has become unchristian is the sole living and convincing evidence that even today Christianity still has a real chance for the future.'[1]

What Rahner perceived to be true for the Roman Catholic Church in Europe, I would contend is equally true for the Church in this country.

The problems

We have to take the winning of new converts seriously; yet this is often one of the weakest points in the life of the local church, even in those churches that have no 'hang-ups' about conversion. The clergy have had little training, and even less experience, in making adult disciples, leading them from a point of interest to a point of commitment to Christ and on into a life of discipleship and service. And if that is true of the leadership it is not unreasonable to assume that it will be even more true of the congregation.

The report of the Archbishops' Commission on Evangelism, published in 1945 under the title, *Towards the Conversion of England: A Plan Dedicated to the Memory of Archbishop William Temple*, still waits to be seriously implemented. Sadly, many of its observations and findings are still as applicable today as they were 40 years ago.

This, for example, is its finding on the training of the clergy in evangelism:

> In view of the immense opportunities open to parochial evangelism, it is alarming to discover how few of the clergy have been given any training in the work of an evangelist, such as in the art of preaching or of personal dealing with enquirers; how few, again, have been used of God to bring a soul to new birth; and how many are embarrassed and tongue-tied when the occasion offers of speaking to individuals about the deepest matters of their eternal welfare.[2]

In the group work at the British Church Growth Association conference in Birmingham (1985) the same inadequacy surfaced. Asked to discuss what problems they had about bringing people to conversion, members admitted to uncertainty about how to proceed, an uncertainty which sprang largely from lack of experience. One minister honestly confessed that he could not recall any occasion when he had personally led someone to faith in Christ. He rejoiced at the conversions that had taken place in his congregation, but he himself had never personally been involved. That, I suspect, would not be uncommon, especially among the clergy of the Church of England. Lack of experience can easily lead to lack of confidence, and the opportunities to make adult converts that still abound in parish life can be missed. If the man or woman at the top is not alert to these opportunities, or does not know how to handle them, it may be tantamount to condemning would-be disciples of Jesus to drifting aimlessly through life, or leaving them to the mercy of the sects.

Leadership role

Fortunately, the responsibility for evangelism does not rest solely with the clergy. In fact, the most effective evangelists are usually ordinary church members. Of course, they need to be motivated, encouraged and guided; and that *is* the responsibility of the clergy. The attitude of the spiritual leader of the local church is crucial in mobilising the church members for evangelism.

There is sometimes a reluctance on the part of the clergy to allow or encourage church members to be involved in evangelism for fear that they may misrepresent the Christian faith. In most cases that is a groundless fear. The Report quotes William Temple as saying:

> It does very little harm if an eager layman talks heresy, provided he shows and imparts a love for the Lord Jesus. It does

great harm if a priest talks orthodoxy so as to make men think the Gospel is dull or irrelevant. How many of our communicants are in fact missionaries in their own parishes? We must turn our congregations into teams of evangelists.[3]

I would endorse that statement whole-heartedly from my own experience over a period of 10 years of releasing untrained church members to lead people to Christ.

Body role

However, I would not wish to give the impression that it is always or only the clergy who frustrate effective evangelism in the local church. As the Report bluntly recognised: 'The chief obstacle [to mobilising and training the laity for evangelism] is that so many church people are only half-converted.'[4] Nevertheless, it urged, quite rightly, that it would be wrong 'to wait till the whole of the church shall be wholly converted. On the contrary, it is by engaging in evangelism that the whole church will be revived and its ardour fanned into flame.'[5] A 'half-converted' church member faced with the questions of an eager enquirer is forced to think through his or her own faith, or lack of it, in a way that no amount of sermons can achieve. Such an encounter sharpens up the issues admirably and is a valuable stimulus to a radical reappraisal of a person's Christian commitment.

The question that the local church so often fails to resolve is precisely how to become a 'converting' agency again. Given the resistance present in both clergy and church members, how can congregations be turned into 'teams of evangelists'? It is in this very practical area that I may be able to make a contribution. What I have to say springs from my experience in two Anglican parishes in the Midlands over a period of 10 years.

Building bridges

A chance remark at a funeral first made me aware of the gap between normal church life and the spiritual questionings of ordinary people. The non-churchgoing population seen through church eyes is often categorised as apathetic or antagonistic. Such generalisations fail to take account of a considerable number of people who have 'spiritual' experiences at one time or another, as the work of Sir Alister Hardy has shown, and ignore many others whose interest in God, or Jesus or the Christian faith ranges from curiosity to a deep quest for spiritual meaning. What is true is that many of them will not look to the institutional church (of whatever brand) to interpret their experience or answer their enquiries. Yet in the normal course of parish ministry we will meet such people, as I did that day at a funeral.

The realisation that, as a church, we had nothing to offer them, no way of really getting alongside them that did not require them to make some move in our direction was profoundly disturbing. Somehow we had to find a way of communicating the good news of Jesus Christ to them. Clearly, only a small percentage of them would respond to an invitation to make any link with the church at that stage. The concept of 'church' creates barriers in people's minds that make it harder for them to respond to the message of Jesus. But whatever we did would have to be within the capabilities of the ordinary members of our church, for they would have to spearhead any advance we made into unknown territory. Furthermore, if whatever we did succeeded in winning people for Christ, we would have to provide stepping-stones for them and not expect them to be able to make instant adjustments to the alien culture of congregational life and worship.

'Good News Down the Street'

Within these constraints, God led us to the scheme that has been fully documented in my Grove Booklet *Good News Down the Street*[6]. I would commend it to you, not as a blueprint for success, but as a starting-point for your own praying and thinking and action in your local church. It has proved its worth in two very different parishes, sociologically speaking. Statistics kept over a 10-year period show that 70% of those who embark on the scheme make a definite commitment to Jesus Christ and only a small minority of those fail to go on to play a full and active part in the life of the church.

Relationship building

The scheme operates in the following way. Whenever a person expresses an interest, however small, in discovering what the Christian faith is about, we encourage them to invite into their home a team of three people from the church for a period of six weeks for an informal discussion that is designed to enable them to think through the implications of the Christian faith for themselves. The discussions follow a simple outline based on the life and teaching of Jesus and lead to an opportunity for people to make a personal commitment to Jesus Christ if that is the point they have reached by the time the course has finished. However, no pressure is put on people to make such a commitment unless they are ready. The aim is to build strong personal relationships so that, whatever the outcome after six weeks, we maintain good links with the people involved. This approach also takes the pressure off church members 'to go for a verdict' in the wrong way. It allows them to relax — after the first week — and express their Christian convictions naturally and with no sense of imposing them on others. It creates a climate in which people can express their views without feeling threatened and can be open to explore together the heart of the gospel.

Opportunities

Invariably, when I talk to people about this scheme they express scepticism about the willingness of non-churchgoers to invite three members from the church into their home for the sort of undertaking I have described. However, if it is presented to them in the way I have described, as an open-ended, no strings attached, non-confrontational opportunity to discuss matters of great importance, many people are happy to take up such an offer. Let me give you three examples that occurred in the parish during one week. I hasten to add that this doesn't happen *every* week!

First, a woman of about 30 came to the vicarage in some distress. I was out at the time and my wife chatted to her. Her next-door neighbours are Jehovah's Witnesses and, seizing upon this woman's interest in religion, they had begun to do Bible studies with her during the day, while her husband, a detective, was at work. The husband, who told me that he goes to church once a year — on Remembrance Sunday! — was getting increasingly disturbed by some of the things being taught by the Witnesses, especially as they affected family life and the education of the children, Christmas, and blood transfusions. He had been putting pressure on his wife to break with them. Hence the turmoil which brought her to the vicarage. I arranged to go and see her and her husband to talk things through. The outcome was that he would be happy to have a team from the church come and do the course with him and his wife.

Second, a routine visit to a couple in their mid-thirties enquiring about baptism for their new-born baby uncovered a real desire on the part of both parents to know more about God. The husband's interest in the Christian faith had been stimulated by a Christian at work who had greatly impressed him by being a really good person to work with. Both he and his wife admitted to moments when they thought about the meaning of life and wondered about God. Neither of them had been to church for 15 years or more. They were looking forward to receiving a team, delighted to have this chance to talk about the spiritual dimension to life.

Third, a woman in her thirties, recently deserted by her husband who went off with her best friend, leaving a boy of 10 and a girl of 7, enquired about having the children baptised. Her husband had refused to allow them to be baptised. When I visited the home I discovered that she was receiving a great deal of caring support from a couple in the congregation

who had been involved with her husband through Scouting. I also discovered that the night before I called she had had a vivid experience of the
numinous, which had left her feeling quite exhilarated, laughing and crying
all at once. Understandably, she did not know what to make of it. When the
Spirit of God is at work, all sorts of unusual things happen. A team
arranged to visit her during the day while the children were at school.

Be prepared

I mention these three cases because they are typical of the sort of opportunities that come the way of most clergy from time to time. I mention
them to encourage you to make sure that your churches are mobilised to
seize such opportunities when they arise, as they surely will. Ten years ago
I would not have known how best to meet the needs of those three homes
— certainly not all at once! Now I rejoice in the knowledge that through
the ministry of teams of ordinary men and women from the congregation,
in each case they receive what they are looking for, to the glory of God.

Notes

1 Karl Rahner, *The Shape of the Church to Come* (SPCK: London, 1974), p 34.
2 *Towards the Conversion of England: A Plan Dedicated to the Memory of
   Archbishop William Temple* (Church Assembly: Westminster, 1945), p 45.
3 *ibid*, p 56.
4 *ibid*, p 54.
5 *ibid*, p 54.
6 Michael Wooderson, *Good News Down the Street*. Grove Pastoral Studies
   Booklets no 9 (Grove Books: Bramcote, 1982).

10
the role of the home

MALCOLM SAUNDERS

The second practical chapter in this symposium looks at conversion in homes. Traditionally the influence of the home has been strong in building up the church in this country, but this influence has declined somewhat in recent years. The opportunities are still there, however, and need to be grasped.

Malcolm Saunders was the vicar of St Columba's, Corby in Northants, for 18 years until in 1984 he became the National Director for Evangelism Explosion, which is based in Southampton. He draws on his experience of home evangelism by teams and church members as well as the 'Teach and Reach' programme of Evangelism Explosion. He gives a number of practical hints on bridging the gaps between church and home today.

If we are to be effective in our attempts to lead people into a living faith in Jesus when in their homes, we need to recognise and work with the factors that make this a somewhat different exercise from conversion efforts when they take place in a church building, a secular hall, or a sports stadium. Undergirding all our evangelistic activity there always needs to be serious prayer and thoughtful training. Whereas there should always be mutual support in prayer between members of the Lord's family, when some know that on a particular occasion they will be attempting to bring the challenge of the gospel to the lives of particular people, then it is valuable if others support them in prayer in a special way. Just as troops in a conventional battle look for air cover, so those taking up an evangelistic role on behalf of their churches need prayer. Further, the troops themselves must be adequately trained to attempt the tasks entrusted to them. We are not in the business of conquest and killing, but of liberation and life. How much more carefully then should the Lord's people prepare themselves for the enormous privilege of being ambassadors for Christ.

This practical chapter is offered as a small contribution towards that training task. We shall attempt to think through some of the distinctive factors involved in trying to lead people to conversion in their own homes.

The home setting

First, the home is familar ground to them. It is their territory, very literally. They have chosen the wallpaper, the carpets, the curtains, the contents of the room, at least in large measure. By and large, it is they who feel comfortable with that setting. We may not like their choice, or the combination, but it is what they are reasonably happy with.

Second, to them it is the real world. It is where family discussions and arguments have taken place, and where any decisions over Christianity will have to be lived out. It is not an outing they are on, whether to a local church, or by coach for an hour to a sports stadium. This place, their home, represents a large slice of reality for them.

A third area of distinctiveness lies in the fact that talking will have to be in conversational form. The set address which is appropriate to a group setting will be out of place here. We must give more attention to this point when we consider the evangelists who go with the gospel.

All these can be distinct advantages. If they do not strike us as being to our advantage when we first think of them, then we must use judo tactics, in which we consider how to turn the force of the apparent disadvantage into an advantage.

But there are some factors which usually do function as distractions. We have to be aware of them, and look for means of neutralising them. TV is sometimes more of a distraction to visitors then to the visited. Ways of handling it range from ignoring it, to unilaterally switching it off! Children stay up later and longer than ever before, or so it seems, and telephones insist on ringing at the wrong times. All this we must take in our stride, recognising that no situation is ever perfect, and sometimes imperfections aid concentration. Think of all those who sat in the rain at Mission England meetings! Think of Jesus teaching at Mary and Martha's home in Bethany, interrupted by Martha's questions about Mary's lack of concern for household responsibilities!

The hearers

The biggest difference between stadium and home is probably the number listening. Churches and church leaders must take their own decisions over the value of ones and twos, especially if they are sending more than one visitor. But often we have the privilege of sharing the gospel with both husband and wife together, and perhaps also with older children. We can move away from some of the problems of individualism and challenge the family unit.

The relationship between hearers and evangelists will have to be personal, even though they may never have met previously. We are there with our hosts' permission and can only keep going with Christian topics by their approval. Happily, a measure of friendship and rapport can be built up over general conversation of half-an-hour to an hour. Experiences can be exchanged, points of interest to the hosts can be pursued, and simply and naturally the Christian person's testimony to the value of having received eternal life can be described. But in all this the attention of the hosts must be retained, especially if it seems appropriate to be sharing specifically Christian teaching. With a group the speaker can keep going even though he may lose the interest of one or two, or even more. But when eyes go back to the TV, or the evening paper, or hearers just get up and wander off, then content that retains the attention is all the more important.

In the home the content of what is being discussed should be varied according to the needs and the understanding of those hearing. Most people will say so if they disagree, or ask for more explanation if they want it, in a way that is rare or impossible during group evangelism. People may accept very readily that they are sinners by God's standards, or imperfect even by their own. On the other hand they may stress most vehemently that they have never done anyone any harm, and have always lived a 'good life'. The evangelist must be ready therefore either to shorten or to expand his material on the nature of human beings, and similarly with much else of his gospel content.

Perhaps the most significant factor about taking the gospel into people's homes at the present time is that very many people in Britain are open to our going, and are open to hearing what we have to say about the gospel. Clearly most will reject or delay a decision, as the parables lead us to expect, but there will be some for whom this is God's time, and who will rejoice to come into a living faith in Jesus Christ as Saviour and Lord.

The evangelists

By the term 'evangelists' we mean those who go into homes with the intention, if appropriate, of attempting to lead others into a personal faith. They will function as evangelists to their hearers. Whether they have also the gift of an evangelist in the New Testament sense is another matter. They are those prepared to 'do the work of an evangelist', to pick St Paul's phrase to Timothy, in this particular situation. There may be only one of them, as in many situations, but if a local church is serious about helping its members to bear their witness verbally as well as visually, then it will want to set up some pattern of training course. 'Evangelism Explosion' or 'Teach and Reach' is obviously such a course, but others exist, and no doubt others will come into being. But if more than one person goes on the visit from the church, then there is the possibility of practical training experience. Since the home calls for a conversational style of presentation, then two or even three people are quite acceptable as the evangelistic team. Inevitably one will speak more, and any others on the team can learn as apprentices by watching and hearing a more experienced person at work. This is how we teach so many crafts and skills, by a combination of learning the theory and watching the practice. Why not apply this to the matter of speaking to others about Jesus? Or indeed to many other tasks and roles in the life of our churches?

A further possibility arises out of the training situation that the conversational approach makes possible. This is that any Christian person can be involved. The long-standing believer can acquire new dimensions to a long-standing skill, and the newest convert can share the joy of new-found faith without needing to feel he or she has to know a lot. Often it is the new believer who makes the biggest impact on the doubtful. But all Christians can become involved in faith-sharing.

As the conversation proceeds, two further factors need to be borne in mind. First, there will be a constant assessment possible of the reaction of the hearers. Whether this is encouraging or discouraging will clearly vary, but at least our evangelists will have a basis of knowledge on which they can decide how to proceed next. And any not directly and immediately involved in the talking can direct their silent prayer to the areas most in need. Many an evangelistic team member has been deeply in prayer while rocking the baby, playing 'Snakes and Ladders' with the six-year-old, or even doing the ironing for a harassed mum.

Finally, there is the need for clear objectives on the part of the evangelists. With so many optional routes for the conversation to go, and so much variation that might be called for in a particular situation, it would be all too easy to let the conversation waffle on without convering much significant ground. What is needed is a clear, simple outline of areas that need to be covered if it is going to be meaningful to ask anyone whether they are ready to receive God's gift of eternal life. We need to know what we should like the conversation to include. But if we have no clear objectives we cannot be surprised if nothing worthwhile emerges.

From home to church

If the people we are visiting already have a link with our church, we shall want to deepen and strengthen that link in whatever ways are appropriate. If they are already linked to another church, we shall still want to take whatever opportunities we have to talk with them about the gospel, but we shall probably be encouraging them to pursue those existing links more seriously. The decision to change churches should be prompted by the Holy Spirit, not induced by us. But if people do not have a live church link, then we shall want to encourage them into our own fellowship. This will be so even where there is no profession of faith made, but it will be all the more important if they have responded positively to our presentation of the gospel. The church is a part of the gospel. And if our church and its life is not good news in itself then we need to re-examine its life and worship.

For new believers both worship and fellowship, however expressed, are essential ingredients for growth. Even though home groups may serve both functions in part, there still needs to be the sharing in the wider life and more rounded worship of the whole company of believers. So we must ask: Is our church conscious of outsiders? Is it geared for people with little or no background, or does it unconsciously exclude those who are not full members of the club? This can be done in a variety of ways: for example, no announcement of hymn or chorus numbers, no page numbers given if a printed order of service is followed, no announcement about what can happen for children in the service, no indication that non-members are welcome to the mid-week activities, no mention of the coffee which 'club' members enjoy at the end, and so on. If visitors and newcomers are made to feel welcome, they can probably cope with our in-house references and even our way-out language: whether Tudor English, pseudo-hippie, or even the language of Sion.

In essence we must ask, does our church look outwards or inwards? Towards growth, which must mean that newcomers are welcomed, helped and re-invited, or towards maintaining the status quo? Some churches give the feeling that they are quite happy as they are, that they do not want more members, and indeed that a serious growth would be a distinct embarrassment. If your church building is often full up now, what would you do with another 100 regular worshippers? Have an expensive building programme? Or split up the cosy fellowship by having a second service? And do the existing members want to cope with another 100 sets of potential relationships?

In this section we have focussed mainly on the expression of the church's life at its main worship service. We must never forget that the church is living people, living to God's glory in a complicated world where many issues must be faced. But if the present congregation will not welcome people in on a Sunday, then they are most unlikely to welcome them in on weekdays. The sharing of life and the consequent mutual up-building are unlikely to come from a congregation that is self-centred on Sundays.

'Headline' conclusions

Let us go into homes, many of us, with the Good News about Jesus. People are there, in their homes, even though not flocking in to our churches. Many Christians, of all ages, both physical and spiritual, can be involved. There are few 'extras'. No committees, no publicity, little expense, although commitment, training and prayer are always needed as in any evangelistic enterprise.

The people of England are still open to hearing about God. This may not be so true in 10 years' time, but today is a time of tremendous opportunity. May our churches see it and seize it, to the glory of God.

11
learning from the past for the future

ROY POINTER

Dr Roy Pointer is a Baptist minister who has been Church Growth Consultant for the Bible Society since 1979 and is currently Chairman of the British Church Growth Association. He is now Director for Church Training for the Bible Society and has written a number of books and articles including 'Tell What God has Done' and 'How Do Churches Grow?'

In this chapter he looks at the past, at the present, and towards the future. He studies the current experience of conversion in the UK today, especially as found in crusade evangelism in the recent Missions both to London and to England. He then explores the possible lessons to be learned from this experience for the future.

He shows that although church attendance in the UK has dropped rapidly in recent years there are still large numbers who claim to believe in God and who call themselves religious; and therefore a context for fruitful evangelism does exist. He challenges the Church to take seriously the need for conversion growth and to reverse the trends of recent years.

Introduction

Peter Brierley's chapter and study of conversion surveys, particularly the survey carried out for the Evangelical Alliance in 1968, makes a good starting-point. The purpose of the survey was described fully in the preface. The Evangelical Alliance Commission on Evangelism felt the need quite early in its deliberations for precise and documented information of the various ways used by God to bring people to faith in him. There was limited value in the largely subjective impressions of evangelists, workers and ministers.[1]

The Commission, therefore, expressed the need for an objective foundation of facts on which to base its assessment of the performance of evangelistic efforts in this country, and it cautioned against placing too much value upon the 'subjective impressions' of Christian workers.

In this chapter I will attempt to avoid too many 'subjective impressions' and use the results of surveys to provide us with objective facts to describe the possible way forward for Britain. However, we need to note two important points. First, the surveys that have been undertaken and the great emphasis on crusade evangelism in the last few years will inevitably bias the chapter toward this means of conversion. Second, I have mainly used research gathered in England with occasional data from the UK, as if it related to the same peoples. For the general purposes of this chapter I believe this is an acceptable procedure.

The Evangelical Alliance survey

In 1966, 20 years ago, the National Assembly of Evangelicals, sponsored by the Evangelical Alliance, passed a resolution worded as follows:

> In view of the urgent spiritual need of the nation, this assembly:
> 1. Dedicates itself anew to the task of evangelism, recognizing its needs for a Scriptural experience of the direction and dynamic of the Holy Spirit.
> 2. Calls for the setting up of a Commission on Evangelism, which will prayerfully consider and recommend the best means of reaching the unchurched masses at national, local and personal levels, bearing in mind the need to co-ordinate existing endeavours where possible and specifically to promote a new emphasis on personal evangelism.[2]

As we have already seen, this Commission on Evangelism called for the survey in order to carry out its assignment.

I have turned to this survey for two reasons. First, as it tests by research the means of conversion, the survey provides a list of means used by God to bring about conversion in the past and therefore a helpful grid to evaluate conversion today and tomorrow in Britain. And second, the report of the Commission on Evangelism was generally unsympathetic to crusade evangelism, which many see as an important means of conversion today and may still be used effectively tomorrow.

The means of conversion

As Peter Brierley has already shown, 33% were unable to point to an actual point of conversion.

The Evangelical Alliance survey published the following table for the means of conversion for the two-thirds who claimed to have a definite conversion experience (see Chapter 8). We ought to note that it was limited to interviewees converted in England, and that some of the people interviewed had been converted as long ago as 1884!

These facts obviously affect and limit the range of means used in the past 100 years. This is probably reflected, for example, in the low percentages converted through modern media such as film and radio.

Means of Conversion	% of 2,590 people
1 In a church context	30%
2 Spasmodic efforts such as a camp, mission etc	22%
3 Through personal witness	15%
4 Through a professional evangelist	13%
5 Regular youth work including Sunday school	10%
6 Alone or by Bible reading	5%
7 Through a film	3%
8 Through radio or literature	2%

**Table 1: Means of Conversion
from the Evangelical Alliance Survey[3]**

Before we leave the subject of the means of conversion, we should note that the list is of means that had 'the greatest influence' in bringing about conversion. Many had been influenced by a variety of means.

Criticisms of crusade evangelism

A section of the report that examined crusade evangelism presented a detailed evaluation of the statistics of the Earl's Court 1966 Billy Graham crusades. It expressed a number of concerns and made several recommendations. In general, the report appeared negative toward crusade evangelism. The evaluation was preceded by the following paragraph:

> Here again, as always in this matter of evangelism, we face a
> very difficult problem of evaluation. Much of the evidence is
> partial and contradictory. People form strong impressions,
> and opinions become substituted for fact. Large organisations

speak with different voices through different spokesmen.
Where a strong sense of mission confronts great frustration,
any area of hope quickly becomes a launch-pad for fantasy.[4]

The report concluded:

> In general, the Commission noted that Crusades of this kind
> made an impression predominantly on young people and
> within that age group on a significantly higher proportion of
> girls than boys. Their impact in the section of the community
> which is normally untouched by the churches is hard to mea-
> sure, and opinions differ. The nature of the impact made by
> such large meetings and the need for the message to be
> addressed primarily to a general audience made the Commis-
> sion look with concern at the percentages of children of
> twelve and under who responded to the appeal.[5]

Nevertheless, under 'Methods to be Considered' for future evangelism
in Britain, crusade evangelism headed the list, but with further reserva-
tions and some recommendations. The particular benefits of crusades are
listed, the point that crusade evangelism accounts for only a small proportion of all conversions is made, and the following disquiet about the
method for the 1970s is stated thus: 'The expressed dissatisfaction
centres in the inadequate understanding of the enquirer about the nature
of the appeal and the limited counselling given afterwards.[6] In the light of
such adverse criticism it was obviously vital that the recent Mission to London and Mission England were thoroughly researched. As a member of the
Executive Committee of Mission to London I am happy to report that this
Mission has been most thoroughly analysed.[7]

MARC Europe conducted a survey of the counsellor forms, returned by
counsellors from the regional missions of Mission to London in the autumn
of 1983, and from the Queen's Park Rangers central mission in the sum-
mer of 1984. In 1984–85 the Bible Society's survey of the actual enquirers at the 1983 regional missions took a representative sample of the
counsellor forms and questioned the enquirers themselves. This is, I
believe, unique. Thus a year after the regional missions of 1983 the Bible
Society had completed a survey of response to the crusade evangelism of
that year. This helps our understanding of conversion today in Britain.

Conversion today in Britain

In the context of overall British church decline we might be forgiven for
believing that there are no conversions taking place in the UK today. The

1970s was another decade of decline, when British churches lost 1,000,000 members and 2,500 ministers, and when 1,000 churches were closed.

However, while overall church decline continues, a study of the 1979 data gathered from churches in England by the Nationwide Initiative in Evangelism discovered that some churches of every denomination were growing and that churches grow in every English county. This research was published in *Prospects for the Eighties, Vol 2*.[8] But was this numerical growth the result of conversions? In order to answer this question we must look briefly at the way churches grow in numbers.

Basic Church Growth analysis classifies the various ways that churches add members.

Biological growth: when the children of Christian parents come to faith and join the church. They are confirmed or baptised and are formally recognised as responsible members of their churches.

Incidentally, one of the great problems of the British church is that so many of the mainline churches are essentially structured to recruit by biological growth and have yet to learn how to recruit by conversion growth.

Transfer growth: when Christians transfer their membership from one church and join another, either because they have moved to a new area or become dissatisfied and joined a neighbouring church.

Restoration growth: when lapsed Christians are restored to faith and active church membership.

Conversion growth: when those outside the church are brought to repentance and faith in Jesus Christ as Lord and Saviour and become active church members.

Conversion, in the sense in which we have been and are considering it, affects both biological and conversion growth.

To return to my original question: Are conversions taking place in the UK today? I want to answer with a resounding yes! And I am convinced by statistics as well as stories.

According to the *UK Christian Handbook (1985/86)*,[10] the House Church Movement has grown from 60,000 to 180,000 in five years. Was this due to conversion growth? In the early days most of the growth was by transfer growth. A few years ago even the House Church leaders themselves were saying 90% of the people who joined them came from other churches. However, the House Church Movement is now developing 'Church Growth Eyes'. They see the missionary task that is before them and are boldly moving out with evangelistic zeal and fervour. They expect to recruit significant numbers by conversion growth. But of course conversions take place in all denominations. Some years ago I was teaching a course at Lytham St Anne's in Blackpool when a retired New York policeman told me, 'I was brought up a Roman Catholic but recently I met these Baptists and they loved me, and I came to know Jesus, they're wonderful!' What he did not know was that the week before I had been teaching a course in Guildford when a Roman Catholic lady had come up to me and said, 'You know, I was brought up a Baptist and then I met these Roman Catholics, and they loved me and then I found Jesus!'

And conversions are still taking place through all the ways mentioned earlier. I hear so many testimonies that I could provide contemporary examples for each means of conversion listed in the Evangelical Alliance survey and others beside. However, I must avoid giving my 'subjective impressions' and turn to conversions that have taken place more recently through crusade evangelism.

Conversions through Mission England and Mission to London

The years 1983 to 1985 saw the completion of three years of intensive crusade evangelism in England. Stadium attendances at Mission to London and Mission England were as follows:

	Attendance	Enquiries	% Response
MTL Autumn 1983	190,450	7,372	3.9
MTL Summer 1984	267,685	16,322	6.1
ME Summer 1984	1,026,600	96,982	9.5
ME Summer 1985	257,900	26,131	10.1
Total	1,742,635	146,807	8.4

Table 2: Attendance and Response at MTL and ME[10]

In order to discover the number of conversions through these major missions we may examine the categories of response by the 146,807 enquirers. We must not forget that these figures are based only upon stadium attendances and no account is taken of video or TV live link meetings which were attended by at least another 300,000 people. There were four basic categories of response.

Acceptance: people who made a profession of faith in Jesus Christ for the very first time.

Rededication: Christians who were rededicating their lives to Christ.

Assurance: Christians who were seeking assurance of salvation.

Other: people who came forward for a variety of reasons. Perhaps they wanted to know more about Christianity, or they had personal or domestic problems. They may or may not have been Christians.

Table 3, showing the proportions responding, further helps us in our pursuit of conversions through Mission England (1984 and 1985) and Mission to London (1983 and 1984). The Bible Society survey of response is in the final column.

	(Back) ME ('84)	(Brierley) MTL ('83)	(Brierley) MTL ('84)	(Barley) BS
Acceptance	56%	55%	57%	43%
Rededication	17%	25%	22%	31%
Assurance	14%	10%	8%	12%
Other	13%	10%	13%	13%

Table 3: Categories of Response at MTL and ME[11]

Notice that, apart from the Bible Society survey, they are all very similar. Between 55–57% of enquirers were first time professions of faith. The Bible Society survey was of enquirers and took place one year after the actual Mission to London. A sample of those who responded in 1983 was contacted. Their perception of their response differed from that recorded by their counsellors. The figures show that the ratio of first time professions of faith to rededications was significantly different. Instead of 55% the Bible Society survey found 43%, and rededications had changed from 25% to 31%.

It is still significant, though, that 43% of enquirers knew precisely what they had done a year after the event. They had repented of their sins and believed in Jesus Christ as their Lord and Saviour; they had been converted.

If we take the counsellor figures, then 56% of 146,807 — or 82,000 enquirers — accepted Christ. If we take the year later self-perceived percentage of 43% of enquirers, then 63,000 people were converted through these missions. And we have taken no account of the people who attended the video relays, or the satellite meetings, or who were converted before or after the missions. I have not counted, for example, the Hell's Angel who was converted and witnessed to his gang and led five other gang members to Christ! Let us take the minimum, conservative estimate given above. This means there were at least 63,000 conversions between 1983 and 1985 through Mission to London or Mission England.

To see the significance of this number of converts we need to compare this with the size of a few denominations. The *UK Christian Handbook (1985/86)* listed only 65,000 members of the Salvation Army, and only

64,000 Christian Brethren. There are only 62,500 Welsh Independents; the Assemblies of God have 60,000 and the Scottish Episcopalians have a mere 38,000![12]

Bible Society research indicates that 8 out of 10 of the 63,000 converts were already attending church so the impact of these conversions will be seen largely in the renewal of many churches rather than immediate numerical church growth. Nevertheless we need to be very grateful and full of praise for what God has done through these great missions, and for all conversions taking place today. But what about conversion tomorrow?

Conversion tomorrow in Britain

The response to the major missions, the growth of the House Church Movement, the very many testimonies of growing churches and individual conversions are all factors that convince me that the United Kingdom has been brought to a period of great receptivity to the gospel. This is God's doing, and this is the British church's harvest time.

There are over 50,000 local churches in the British Church and any concern for conversion tomorrow must endeavour to help each one bring home the harvest. But how?

Expect conversion growth

We have already noted the serious decline of the British church and the various means of numerical growth in local churches. It is therefore imperative that conversion growth is what the Church throughout the United Kingdom should be praying and working for. How is this to be achieved? Conversion growth in churches is achieved when they, the people of God, make an impact on the unconverted with the Word of God, under the direction and empowering of the Spirit of God.

British Christians also need to be reminded that the activity of the Holy Spirit in evangelism is not only upon the people and Word of God, but also upon the unconverted. God's desire for Britain has not lessened through the years. God still desires that British people turn to Jesus Christ and be converted. He is *now* at work by his Holy Spirit, in the hearts and minds of countless thousands of people throughout the British Isles. It is his harvest, and by his grace it is *our* opportunity.

In this context of great receptivity to the gospel, British churches should have similar faith convictions for their evangelism as held by missionary Lester Knoll, in Papua New Guinea.

The conviction that the Spirit of God has already been at work. Every local church should fervently believe that the Spirit of God is at work in their community or parish and people are prepared to hear and heed the gospel. Millions of British people may be won for Christ.

The conviction that personal conversion is essential.   British people need to be converted to Christ. Far too many people, even in the Church, believe that being British is synonymous with being Christian. A survey conducted for Mission to London[13] revealed that people in London were willing to be called 'unchurched' but resented being classified as non-Christian. 'Conversion' should return to the Church's and Britain's vocabulary as well as experience.

The conviction that the Father desires to express his love personally to each person.   While we recognise the corporate dimensions of conversion, individuals need to have Jesus Christ reigning over their lives and acknowledge and confess that Jesus Christ is Lord. The core of Christianity is a personal response and relationship to God as Father through his Son.

The conviction that when the Spirit breaks through to consciousness, there will be evident signs of changed lives.   Paul declared, 'If anyone is in Christ, he is a new creation; the old has gone, the new has come!' (II Cor 5:17). The converted person has a transformed mind, Spirit-controlled emotions and changed lifestyle.

If these four convictions governed all evangelism in the UK there would be much conversion growth.

Identify windows of receptivity

If we want to see conversion tomorrow we really must begin where people are today, religiously speaking, in the United Kingdom. Paul at Antioch (Acts 13:16), or at Lystra (Acts 14:17) or Athens (Acts 17:22), began where people were and we should do the same. We ought to begin by recognising where they are in relation to the British church.

Sadly this is often not the case. I was surprised recently by a prayer letter from an organisation which claims that 40 million British people have no regular contact with the Church. This is nonsense and not only fails to face the facts but panders to the designs of other religions and sects who are very active in the United Kingdom and want to belittle the role and status of Christianity in the nation.

Two recent surveys of British religion reveal surprising levels of church contact and religious beliefs. The *European Values Survey (EVS)*[14] which is a survey of moral and religious values in Europe, and a survey conducted by Bible Society called *Attitudes to Bible, God and Church (ABGC)*,[15] show the context in which we are seeking to convert people today.

There were approximately 43 million adults (over 14) in the UK at the time of the surveys (1981–82). On any given Sunday, according to the *Attitudes to Bible, God and Church* survey, about 15% or 6.5 million attended church.[16]

The *ABGC* survey also revealed that 22% attend church at least once a month and may be termed 'regular attenders'.[17] At Easter 30% of the adult population attend church and 40% attend at Christmas.[18] Gallup discovered that 58% of British people consider themselves 'religious' and 76% 'believe in God'.[19] From these figures the following table emerges:

	Survey	% of Adult Population	Total
Average Sunday attendance	(ABGC)	15%	6.5m
Regular attenders	(ABGC)	22%	9.5m
Easter attenders	(ABGC)	30%	13m
Christmas attenders	(ABGC)	40%	17m
Religious	(EVS)	58%	25m
Believe in God	(EVS)	76%	32m
Others	(EVS)	100%	43m

Table 4: Religious Belief/Church Attendance in Great Britain

Surprisingly large numbers of British people attend church and 58% are prepared to say that they are 'religious'. Of course this religious belief is not necessarily Christianity, but despite the onslaught of secularism and all the reasons for not believing, British people are saying they have a religious world-view. A total of 76% are prepared to say that 'I believe in God.' Of course much, if not most, is mechanistic rather than theistic, but nevertheless it is a most remarkable statistic.

The Bible Society sample indicated that 81% of British adults (35 million) are in touch with churches for the 'rites of passage'.[20] These are the religious ceremonies associated with birth, puberty, marriage, and death. With so many British people attending churches for the Christian festivals and for these life-related ceremonies, there are great opportunities for evangelism. All of these occasions are 'windows of receptivity' when people are asking religious questions and many are open to hear the gospel. If we cannot preach the Good News of the Kingdom at such times as these, we really have run out of ideas!

Equip the people of God with the Word of God

We have suggested that in the UK there is great receptivity to the gospel, and it is therefore a time of great opportunity for the churches. If the British church wants to grasp these opportunities and see much and rapid conversion growth it should use evangelistic means which maximise the ability of the people of God to make an impact on the unconverted with the Word of God — oral and written — under the direction and empowering of the Spirit of God. This may be done in the following ways.

Evangelise a Christian's network

Many opportunities arise for witness in daily life. A believer is at the centre of a circle of influence: at work, at play, at church, at school, in the home. All of these contacts in these areas provide many opportunities for Christian witness and service. This is the *spontaneous evangelism* that results from the overspill of the Holy Spirit. Where the Church is growing rapidly this kind of evangelism is the norm.

Use the windows of receptivity

We must maximise the use of the Word of God and contact with the people of God when the unconverted come to church. We should take full advantage of the windows of receptivity and meet people sensitively with the gospel at their publicly declared point of need. They need, particularly at these times, the embrace of God's people and News that is Good.

And as we have seen, these windows of receptivity are not only related to the rites of passage but also the passage of time. Time is passing and man needs to mark the seasons. It is not without significance that the Church has overlaid pagan festivals with its own. All cultures are religiously engaged in the marking and pacing of time, and this is symptomatic of man's quest for religious meaning and for God. For this reason 17 million British people are in church for the winter festival. This is a tremendous opportunity and we must not waste it!

Use mass evangelism to reach the masses

We should acknowledge what crusade evangelism and other programmes of mass evangelism can achieve, especially in great urban centres. The problem of urbanisation is with us. Only seven urban centres had a population of more than 5 million in 1950 — New York, London, Paris, Germany's Rhine-Ruhr complex, Tokyo/Yokohama, Shanghai and Buenos Aires. Today, however, 34 cities boast more than 5 million residents. By the year 2025 the UN projects there will be 93, and 80 of these will be in the American nations. Some cities will be 'mega-cities' with 30 million residents by the turn of the century. The great challenge of today and tomorrow is how do you reach such large numbers of people? In many parts of the world the Church is using and developing a great variety of mass evangelistic programmes to reach the masses.

Of course, crusade evangelism is only one means of reaching large numbers and it needs to be considerably improved to effectively reach the 'unchurched'. Other means that the Church is using today, and will undoubtedly use tomorrow, include the electronic media and the mass distribution of the Scriptures. Where these 'blanket' approaches have the facility for those who hear to respond, they can lead to meaningful contact with the people of God. When they have located the 'Cornelius soul' they can be brought to Christ.

We have the technology and the experience to develop great programmes for harvesting. When these are yielded to the service and purpose of God I believe they have the ability to equip thousands of God's people to use his Word, and bring his harvest home.

With cultural adaption many of these great programmes could be sensitively used throughout the United Kingdom in years to come. We should challenge the whole British Church to unite in such a great evangelistic endeavour. To join together in a programme that seeks, as its primary goal, to bring Britain to its knees before the Cross of Christ.

Conclusion

What is the ultimate goal? I am praying that by the end of this century 30% of the population of these islands will be active members of churches. If that is to happen there will have to be millions converted to Christ in the next 15 years. That is my personal vision for the future of the kingdom of God in Great Britain.

Notes

1 *Background to the Task* (Scripture Union: London, 1968).
2 *On the Other Side* (Evangelical Alliance: London, 1968), p 11.
3 *Background to the Task*, section 20.
4 *On the Other Side*, p 135.
5 *On the Other Side*, p 145.
6 *On the Other Side*, p 168.
7 See Linda Barley, *Let the Whole of London Hear the Voice of God* (Bible Society unpublished report: London, February 1985), which focuses on area missions of 1983; Peter Brierley, *Mission to London, Phase I: Who Responded?* and *Mission to London, Phase II: Who Went Forward?* (MARC Europe: London, 1984 and 1985); Philip Back, *Mission England: What Really Happened?* (MARC Europe: London, 1986).
8 Nationwide Initiative in Evangelism, *Prospects for the Eighties, vol 2: From a Census of the Churches in 1979* (MARC Europe: London, 1983).
9 Peter Brierley, ed, *UK Christian Handbook 1985/86* (MARC Europe: London,

1984), p 114.
10 Brierley, *Mission to London, Phase I*, p 6; *Phase II*, pp 9–10; Back, *op cit*, p 14–16.
11 See Brierley, *Phase I*, p 11; *Phase II*, p 19; Back, *op cit*, p 34; and Barley, *op cit*.
12 *UK Christian Handbook*, pp 111, 114, 116, 117.
13 Consumer attitude discussions prepared as background for advertising strategy for Luis Palau's Mission to London (unpublished: London, 1984).
14 Jan Harrison, *European Values Survey* (Gallup and Bible Society: London, 1982).
15 Jan Harrison, *Attitudes to Bible, God and Church* (Bible Society report: London, 1983).
16 *ibid*, para 5.1.8.
17 *ibid*, para 6.1.8.
18 *ibid*, para 5.1.9.
19 Harrison, *EVS*, para 5.2.2.
20 Harrison, *ABGC*, para 6.1.8.

summary and conclusions

MONICA HILL

The Kingdom is based on relationships between God and man, and between man and man. There would be no Kingdom without the establishing of that central relationship between God and man. Whether explicitly or implicitly each of the contributors to this book recognised this basic truth and has sought to examine how to establish that right relationship with God so that all may enter the Kingdom.

No blueprint

If our examination has demonstrated one thing it is that there is no one formula for 'entering the Kingdom' — no norm, no set pattern of experience or form of words that signifies that a person has obtained the necessary 'qualifications'. Peter Brierley in his chapter gives an extensive list of people who have come to the experience of conversion along different roads. Krailsheimer describes the conversion experience of 13 very different converts in his book *Conversion*.[1]

Limiting the Kingdom

It becomes obvious as we discover the wide variety of interpretations of conversion in the world church — described by Arthur Glasser in his chapter — that we in Europe have often narrowed conversion into a middle-class Western Protestant concept which is removed from its biblical roots — as described by George Carey. Too often this has been an excuse for excluding others from God's kingdom. We are unable or unwilling to comprehend how people who have not had a similar experience to our own can be acceptable in the Kingdom.

For example, a couple known to me who had been in ministry for a number of years applied for membership of the local church nearest their home. They were quizzed by the elders; the test applied took no account of the fruits of their ministry or even of their present state of faith but was mainly to see if they could describe their conversion experience of many years before in acceptable terms. Another woman from a similar background was refused membership of the same church because she was unable to describe her 'turning to Christ' in terms acceptable to the elders — despite a lifetime of Christian commitment.

This underlines the important point illustrated in this book: that a stereotyped conversion (as demanded by some sectors of the evangelical church) has become a stumbling block at the entrance to the Kingdom. The open portal supposedly welcoming new believers into the Kingdom — as embodied in the Good News — may be blocked by legalism. Again, we must emphasise that this is one of the consequences of the concept of conversion drifting away from its biblical foundations.

Analysis

We need to remind ourselves that there *is* only one Kingdom and it is the same Kingdom open to all, worldwide. The statisticians produced tables to help us understand the facts of the situation, particularly in England and the United Kingdom. Both Peter Brierley and Roy Pointer drew lessons from past figures which could prove useful in future planning. They both highlighted the importance of the Church's fringe. Further deductions show the mobility of Christians in England in recent years, resulting in a concentration on transfer rather than conversion growth. Roy Pointer has also undertaken an analysis of the missions of 1983 and 1984 in England, and the effectiveness of crusade evangelism in the light of decisions recorded there and in previous surveys.

Structure and strategy

Jeffrey Harris's contribution shows us how easily institutions can reverse the order of priorities in local, national and denominational situations. Structures must not be allowed to become the masters of the strategy but should flow out of strategies, which in turn should develop from aims and goals, not the other way round.

In practice

The two essentially practical chapters by Michael Wooderson and Malcolm Saunders concentrate upon every member becoming involved in sharing their faith and bringing others to Christ through conversion either in the context of family and home or in the local church. These are only two possible examples; we could have included many other practical and relevant chapters on different methods or starting-points, not just in the British culture at this time, but worldwide.

The need to turn

One of the major conclusions to which the examples point is the need to show the relevance of the gospel to unbelievers — the need for conversion among those for whom in the past it has had no relevance. This involves the breaking down of barriers. It involves giving the gospel a context without diluting the original dynamic.

Arthur Glasser highlights the difference between those who have been brought up as Christians and who thus experience conversion in a protected environment, and those who are converted from outside the Church. To both, the experience is real; but to the latter the changes in values may be more radical and far-reaching. The turning described in this book is *towards* God — enabling us to look at the world through *his* eyes. It is a conversion of priorities. Turning towards God is primary; turning away from old values is secondary.

The poor

Chris Sugden's chapter focuses on the impact of conversion, particularly on the poor, and on what they can teach the Church about the Kingdom. As John Nightingale summarised:

> It is not necessarily that they (the poor) are any better or worse than the rest of us, but they are in most need of good news and often those most ready to receive it. It is a cruel irony that the materially poor of this world are the more likely to have been deprived of the opportunity of hearing the gospel. The poor see things very clearly and differently from the rich; just as they need the gospel so do we need their testimony.[2]

Kingdom values

The emphasis of a number of contributors was on the values of the Kingdom into which we are called by Christ. These values turn worldly values
upside down (see Chapter 1) and help us to live in the Kingdom now. Jesus
was advocating a radical departure from the worldly norm on many issues
such as love, vengeance, sense of self-worth — as well as social structures.
of others in any conversion can only be as catalysts: faith is caught not
taught.

Today as the family in many parts of the world has been weakened we
hardly plumb the depth of meaning when Jesus said that because of the
values of the Kingdom 'they will be divided, father against son' (Luke
12:53). But to understand the impact of this statement we need to
remember that in Jesus' day the family was the core unit of society: to go
against it was unthinkable. Jesus, however, was teaching that the Kingdom is a new kind of society with loyalties that override both legal and
natural putative relationships. Jesus said, 'Whoever does God's will is my
brother and sister and mother' (Mark 3:35). Peter summarised this when
speaking of the mixture of cultures, relationships and races found in the
Church. 'Once you were not a people, but now you are the people of God'
(I Peter 2:10). Commitment to Christ draws men and women of all
backgrounds together and makes them one in Christ. 'There is neither Jew
nor Greek, slave nor free, male nor female, for you are all one in Christ
Jesus' (Gal 3:28).

European secularism

The sometimes secular mindset of the European, who often lacks an
understanding of a spiritual dimension to life, creates a barrier to the
experience of conversion. Conversion will open up the secularist to
spiritual things, but problems arise when he attempts to relate spiritual
values to the reality in which he lives. Conflict is produced when he tries
to work his faith out in a secularist environment, and this often results in
a form of syncretism.

Syncretism

Europeans can see syncretism in the beliefs and practice of people of other
cultures but are often blind to it in their own situation. Lesslie Newbigin
makes reference to the syncretistic European church in which the sec-

ularist world experience is married to the spiritual experience, then intellectualised. Inevitably the spiritual is subjugated to the secular and the authority of spiritual values is reduced so that everything becomes a matter of debate. Transcendental values are experiential and therefore personalised; they are no longer seen as ultimate values beyond challenge. There are no absolutes since all spiritual phenomena are open to debate. Sadly, thus there may arise a 'God is dead' theology — a form of syncretism peculiar to the modern Western church.

Values and facts

Lesslie Newbigin contrasts the world of facts and the world of values, which appear more irreconcilable in Europe than on any other continent. Charles Dickens devoted a whole book, *Hard Times*, to this dichotomy. He illustrated it in his description of Sissy Jupe's schooling. Her father rides and trains horses for a circus, and she values and loves them too. But as girl number 20 in Thomas Gradgrind's class she cannot define a horse in factual terms that will please him. She has not shed the world of feeling and fancy for the world of facts. One of her contemporaries did, however, defining a horse as 'Quadruped, graminiverous, four legs ... sheds coat in spring ... hoofs hard but requiring to be shod with iron ...'[3] The boy missed the *value* of a horse altogether! He had no *experience* of horses except intellectually.

No matter how much intellectual knowledge we have, we only know *about* God until we actually experience him. When experience comes first, then intellect can follow; but it may be more difficult the other way round.

In Britain there has been a tendency to reverse the Great Commission. In this Jesus commanded his followers to 'make disciples of all nations ... then teach them' (Matthew 28:19–20). It is surely a fallacy to think that one can teach the faith first and then hope to make disciples (ie, committed believers) out of those who have come to regard the faith as some kind of examinable subject in an academic curriculum. Jesus' order is the correct one — make disciples first because new believers with a living experience of Christ will then be eager to learn. When Christians accept the place of the experiential then head knowledge can become an aid, not a hindrance, to spiritual growth.

Catalysts

Conversion as the personal encounter of man with God often occurs in crises, when the individual has reached the limit of his human resources. Under these circumstances the Christian evangelist, teacher, or counsellor may play a vital part in helping an individual to open up to God. But the role of others in any conversion can only be as catalysts: faith is caught not taught.

The truth of this statement has been exemplified by church history in Britain since the earliest days of the gospel's arrival on its shores. The record of Bishop Aidan who in the sixth century preached 'the true faith' to the Northumbrians with the 'desire that the folk should be completely turned to Christ,' shows that although 'he earnestly preached and taught' it was *his example of love* that turned many to Christ.[4]

Spiritual rebirth

Many Christians can point to a particular time of accepting Christ but their one-off experience of conversion may not have changed all their values. But if conversion is true to the biblical pattern of spiritual rebirth, it will change every aspect of a person's life. Such an experience will include repentance and belief as an act of will — of deliberate turning away from worldly commitment, secular pursuits, and even some human loyalties, to put foremost a commitment to Christ and to the values of the Kingdom.

Growing in the Kingdom

A once-off conversion experience is insufficient: God's work in our lives must continue. Even such a full biblical experience of turning, belief, rebirth and entering the Kingdom must be followed by a continual experience of the presence of the living God who sustains spiritual growth to maturity in Christ. Thus the believer will be shielded from the temptation to regard conversion as a one-off, once-in-a-lifetime ephemeral experience that touches the emotional surface for a moment but goes no deeper to produce the fruit of repentance and a lifetime of committed discipleship. General Booth recognised the need for a continual experience of Christ when he refused to allow anybody to give a testimony of the Lord's working in their lives which was more than two weeks old. The experience of entering the Kingdom is the beginning of discipleship.

Total turning

Every area of life needs to be refined by the gospel: this includes personal values and lifestyle. If these remain untouched after someone has entered the Kingdom, there is a danger that in crises he may revert to worldly values — as both Glasser and Newbigin point out.

God's purposes

George Carey notes that the conversion of *individuals* has been the main focus of the Western church; he shows, however, that God intends to bring about a change that affects the whole natural order of creation. Paul saw that 'the whole creation has been groaning as in the pains of childbirth right up to the present time' (Rom 8:22), waiting for the redemptive activity of God.

God's purpose is to harmonise the whole of nature, reconciling and bringing everything into a right relationship with himself. Isaiah sees the completion of God's purpose in the establishment of the new heaven and the new earth where 'the wolf and the lamb will feed together ... They will neither harm nor destroy in all my holy mountain' (Isa 65:25), and where men 'will beat their swords into ploughshares and their spears into pruning hooks. Nation will not take up sword against nation, nor will they train for war any more' (Isa 2:4).

Thus the Kingdom that is revealed in the Bible is not the work of man's hands: a human urban utopia. The Kingdom is God's creation — 'the city with foundations, whose architect and builder is God' (Heb 11:10).

In many ways this study has only begun to touch a vast subject — a subject that needs to be reopened and given serious consideration by Christian leaders. It raises issues of significance for the Church today, especially in Europe. The implications for the Western church are clear. We must cease to regard conversion as a minority pursuit for a few churches within the Body of Christ; we must put it firmly on the agenda of every church. This will happen when we see conversion not in terms of a nineteenth-century revivalist movement but in its basic biblical context as the prerequisite for entering the Kingdom.

Notes

1 A J Krailsheimer, *Conversion* (SCM Press: London, 1980).
2 John Nightingale, 'Reflections on Conversion', *Church Growth Digest*, vol 7 no 2 (British Church Growth Association, winter 1985/86), p 6.
3 Charles Dickens, *Hard Times* (Penguin: Harmondsworth, 1969), p 50.
4 Anno 565 of the *Anglo Saxon Chronicle* trans 1986 by E Gibson.

bibliography

Analytical Greek Lexicon. Samuel Bagster.

Anderson, Gerald, ed. *The Theology of Christian Mission.* SCM Press: London, 1961.

Anglo Saxon Chronicle. Anno 565.

Back, Philip. *Mission England: What Really Happened?* MARC Europe: London, 1986.

Background to the Task. Scripture Union: London, 1968.

Bangkok Assembly 1973. World Council of Churches: Geneva.

Banks, Robert. *The Tyranny of Time.* Paternoster Press: Exeter, 1985.

Barley, Linda. *Let the Whole of London Hear the Voice of God* (unpublished report). Bible Society: London, 1983.

Beasley Murray, G. *Jesus and the Kingdom of God.* Paternoster Press: Exeter, 1986.

Berkhof, Hendrikus. *Christ and the Powers.* Trans J H Yoder. Herald Press: Scottdale, 1962.

Bettenson, H, ed. *Documents of the Christian Church.* Oxford University Press: Oxford, 1954.

Bonino, Jose Miguez. 'Conversion. New Creature and Commitment.' *International Review of Mission.* Vol 72, no 287 (July 1983): pp 324–32.

Bria, Ian. 'Confessing Christ Today.' *International Review of Mission.* Vol 64, no 253 (January 1975): pp 70, 71.

Brierley, Peter. *Mission to London, Phase I: Who Responded?.* MARC Europe: London, 1984.

Brierley, Peter. *Mission to London, Phase II: Who Went Forward?.* MARC Europe: London, 1986.

Brierley, Peter, ed. *UK Christian Handbook 1985/86*. MARC Europe: London, 1984.

Brown, C. *Dictionary of New Testament Theology*. Paternoster Press: Exeter, 1975–78.

Brunner, Emil. *The Great Invitation*. Westminster Press: Philadelphia, 1955.

Burkhardt, N. *The Biblical Doctrine of Regeneration*. Evangelical Monographs no 2. Paternoster Press: Exeter, 1978.

Caird, George Bradford. *Principalities and Powers: A Study in Pauline Theology*. Clarendon Press: Oxford, 1956.

'Christian Witness, Proselytism and Religious Liberty in the Setting of the World Council of Churches.' *Evanston to New Delhi*. Appendix 8. World Council of Churches: Geneva, 1961.

Constitutional Discipline of the Methodist Church. Methodist Publishing House, 1974.

Crossman, Richard. *The God that Failed*. Harper and Row: New York, 1950.

Devanadan, Paul D. 'Called to Witness.' *The Ecumenical Review*. Vol 14, no 2 (January 1962): pp 154–63.

Dickens, Charles. *Hard Times*. Penguin: Harmondsworth, 1969.

Dodd, C H. *The Apostolic Preaching and its Development*. Hodder and Stoughton: London, 1936.

Drucker, Peter. *Management*. Harper and Row: New York, 1974.

Fey, Harold E, ed. *A History of the Ecumenical Movement*. Vol 2. Westminster Press: Philadelphia, 1970.

Ford, Leighton, 'Conversion: God's Climax and Man's Crisis' (unpublished paper). Presented at the Ecumenical Evangelism Conference of the National Council of Churches: Green Lake, Wisconsin, 1967.

Forsyth, P T. *Positive Preaching and the Modern Mind*. Independent Press: London, 1949.

Gospel to the Whole Person, The. TAFTEE: Bangalore.

Hampole. *Psalter*. C 1340.

Harrison, Jan. *Attitudes to Bible, God and Church*. Bible Society: London, 1983.

Harrison, Jan. *European Values Survey*. Gallup and Bible Society: London, 1982.

Hengel, Martin. *Acts and the History of Earliest Christianity*. SCM Press: London, 1979.

Henry, Carl F H and Mooneyham, W Stanley. *One Race, One Gospel, One Task*. Vol 1. Worldwide Publications: Minneapolis, 1967.

Hiebert, Paul G. 'The Flaw of the Excluded Middle.' *Missiology: An International Review*. Vol 10, no 1 (January 1982): pp 35–47.

Hogg, William Richey. *Ecumenical Foundations*. Harper and Brothers: New York, 1952.

Hooft, Willem Visser't. *Has the Ecumenical Movement a Future?*. John Knox Press: Atlanta, 1976.

Hunter, George and McGavran, Donald. *Church Growth Strategies that Work*. Abingdon Press: Nashville, TN, 1980.

Jenkins, David. 'The Church, Bride of Christ, and her Mission.' *Student World*. Vol 50, no 1 (1957): pp 331–37.

Jungmann, J. *The Early Liturgy*. Darton, Longman and Todd: London, 1959.

Kempis, Thomas à. *Imitation of Christ*. C 1430.

Kerr, Hugh T and Mulder, John M. *Conversions: The Christian Experience*. Eerdmans: Grand Rapids, 1983.

Kittel, G. *Theological Dictionary of the New Testament*. Eerdmans: Grand Rapids, 1964–76.

Krailsheimer, A J. *Conversion*. SCM Press: London, 1980.

Lindsell, Harold. *The Church's Worldwide Mission*. Word Books: Waco, 1966.

Loffler, Paul. 'Conversion in an Ecumenical Context.' *The Ecumenical Review*. Vol 19, no 3 (July 1967): pp 252–60.

Loffler, Paul. 'Conversion to God and Men' (unpublished paper). World Council of Churches Division of World Mission and Evangelism: London, August 1964.

Man's Disorder and God's Design. Amsterdam Assembly Series. Vol 2. Harper and Brothers: New York, 1948.

Martos, J. *Doors to the Sacred*. SCM Press: London, 1981.

McGavran, Donald A. *Understanding Church Growth*. Revised edition. Eerdmans: Grand Rapids, 1980.

McGavran, Donald A. 'Wrong Strategy.' *International Review of Mission* (October 1965): pp 451–61.

Milton, John. *Paradise Lost*. 1667.

Nationwide Initiative in Evangelism. *Prospects for the Eighties, vol 2: From a Census of the Churches in 1979*. MARC Europe: London, 1983.

Neill, Stephen. 'The Nature of Salvation.' *The Churchman*. Vol 89 (July–September 1975): pp 225–34.

Newbigin, Lesslie. 'Mission and Missions.' *Christianity Today*. Vol 4, no 22 (August 1, 1960): p 911.

Newbigin, Lesslie. 'The Missionary Dimension of the Ecumenical Movement.' *The Ecumenical Review*. Vol 14, no 2 (January 1962): pp 207–15.

Newbigin, Lesslie. 'One Body, One Gospel, One World.' *The Ecumenical Review*. Vol 11, no 2 (January 1959): pp 143–56.

Newbigin, Lesslie. *The Other Side of 1984*. British Council of Churches: London, 1984.

Newbigin, Lesslie. *Unfinished Agenda*. SPCK: London, 1985.

Nicholls, Bruce. *In Word and Deed. Evangelism and Social Responsibility*. Paternoster Press: Exeter, 1986.

Nightingale, John. 'Reflections on Conversion.' *Church Growth Digest*. Vol 7, no 2. British Church Growth Association (Winter 1985/86): p 6.

Nott, Stephen. *Jesus and Social Ethics*. Grove Booklets, 1984.

Padilla, Rene. *Mission Between the Times*. Paternoster Press: Exeter, 1986.

Padilla, Rene and Sugden, Christopher. *Tests on Evangelical Social Ethics 1974–1983*. Grove Booklets, 1985.

Pocknee, C. *Water and the Spirit*. Darton, Longman and Todd: London, 1967.

Rahner, Karl. *The Shape of the Church to Come*. SPCK: London, 1974.

Salvation Today and Contemporary Experience. World Council of Churches: Geneva, 1973.

Samuel, Vinay and Sugden, Christopher, eds. *Evangelism and the Poor*. Paternoster Press: Exeter, 1984.

Sandstrom, Hakan. *How May We Be Evangelistic in Europe?*. Methodist Home Mission Division, 1974.

Schillebeeckx, Edward. *The Church with a Human Face*. SCM Press: London.

Schlier, Heinrich. *Principalities and Powers in the New Testament*. Herder and Herder: New York, 1961.

Schmaus, M. 'Justification and the Last Things.' *Dogma*. Vol 6 (1977): p 6.

Sharpe, Eric J. 'The Problem of Conversion in Recent Missionary Thought.' *The Evangelical Quarterly*. Vol 41, no 4 (1969): p 221.

Shenk, Wilbert R. ed. *Exploring Church Growth*. Eerdmans: Grand Rapids, 1983.

Shorter, Aylward. *African Christian Theology: Adaptation or Incarnation?*. Maryknoll/Orbis Books, 1977.

Sider, Ronald, ed. *Evangelicals and Development Towards a Theology of Social Change*. Paternoster Press: Exeter, 1981.

Sitler, Joseph A. 'Called to Unity.' *The Ecumenical Review*. Vol 14, no 2 (January 1962): pp 177–87.

Smedes, Lewis B. 'Christian Hope at Accra.' *The Reformed Journal* (November 1974): p 17.

Smith, Eugene L. 'Renewal in Mission.' *Church Growth Bulletin*. Vol 5, no 2 (November 1968): pp 325, 326.

Snyder, Howard. *Liberating the Church*. Inter-Varsity Press: Downers Grove, IL, 1983.

Stott, John R W and Hubbard, David. 'Does Section Two Provide Sufficient Emphasis on World Evangelism?' *Church Growth Bulletin*. Vol 4, no 2 (November 1968): pp 329–33.

Sugden, Christopher. *Radical Discipleship*. Marshalls: Basingstoke, 1981.

Svere, Aslen. '"Reign" and "House" in the Kingdom of God in the Gospels.'

New Testament Studies. Vol 8 (1961): pp 215–40.

Tippett, Alan R. *Verdict Theology in Missionary Theory.* Lincoln Christian College: Lincoln, IL, 1969.

Toffler, Alvin. *The Third Wave.* Pan Books: London, 1980.

Towards the Conversion of England: A Plan Dedicated to the Memory of Archbishop William Temple. Church Assembly: Westminster, 1945.

Transformation, vol 1, no 4 (1984): pp 23–27, 'Social Transformation: The Church in Response to Human Need' (Wheaton, 1983).

Uppsala Report. World Council of Churches: Geneva, 1968.

Van Gennep, Arnold. *The Rites of Passage.* University of Chicago Press: Chicago, 1960.

Vatican II Documents: *Constitution on the Sacred Liturgy (Sacrosanctum concilium)* 9; *Decree on the Church's Missionary Activity (Ad gentes)* 7, 13, 40; *Decree on the Ministry and Life of Priests (Presbyterorum ordinis)* 4, 18; *Decree on Ecumenism (Unitatis redintegratio)* 7, 8.

Verkuyl, Johannes. *Contemporary Missiology.* Eerdmans: Grand Rapids, 1978.

Walker, W. *A History of the Christian Church.* T and T Clark, 1947.

Wallis, Jim. *The Call to Conversion.* Lion: Tring, 1981.

Wesley, John. *The Journal of John Wesley.* Standard edition. Epworth Press, 1938.

Wesley, John. *Works.* Vol 1. 1740.

'Willowbank Report: Gospel and Culture.' *Lausanne Occasional Papers.* no 2. Lausanne Committee for World Evangelization: Charolotte, NC, 1978.

Winter, Ralph. *The Evangelical Response to Bangkok.* William Carey Library: Pasadena, 1973.

Winter, Ralph. 'Ghana: Preparation for Marriage.' *International Review of Mission.* Vol 67, no 267 (1978): p 344.

Wooderson, Michael. *Good News Down the Street.* Grove Pastoral Studies Booklet no 9. Grove Books: Bramcote, 1982.

Wright, C J W. 'The Ethical Relevance of Israel as a State.' *Transformation.* Vol 1, no 4, p 11.